Park Avenue
POTLUCK

The Society of
Memorial Sloan-Kettering Cancer Center

Park Avenue
POTLUCK

RECIPES FROM
New York's Savviest Hostesses

FLORENCE FABRICANT

PHOTOGRAPHS BY BEN FINK

RIZZOLI
NEW YORK

THE SOCIETY OF MEMORIAL SLOAN-KETTERING CANCER CENTER
GRATEFULLY ACKNOWLEDGES CONTRIBUTIONS FROM THE FOLLOWING:
TOWN & COUNTRY AND PAMELA FIORI, EDITOR-IN-CHIEF
TURBOCHEF

First published in the United States of America in 2007 by
Rizzoli International Publications, Inc.
300 Park Avenue South
New York, NY 10010
www.rizzoliusa.com

© 2007 Florence Fabricant and The Society of Memorial Sloan-Kettering Cancer Center.

Photographs © 2007 Ben Fink.

The publisher wishes to gratefully acknowledge the Musée Bouilhet-Christofle and Pepin Press
for their kind permission to reproduce the illustrations contained in this book.

2007 2008 2009 2010 / 10 9 8 7 6 5 4 3 2 1

Distributed in the U.S. trade by Random House, New York

Designed by Patricia Fabricant
Food styling by Melissa Hamilton

Printed in the United States of America

ISBN-10: 0-8478-2989-8
ISBN-13: 978-0-8478-2989-7

Library of Congress Control Number: 2007925275

Dedicated to the patients of
Memorial Sloan–Kettering Cancer Center,
as well as their families and caregivers.

The Society of Memorial Sloan–Kettering Cancer Center

COOKBOOK COMMITTEE

Kelly Forsberg — *Chairman*

Barbara Tollis — *Vice-Chairman*

Wendy Arriz

Muffie Potter Aston

Chesie Breen

Catherine Carey

Annabelle Fowlkes

Jamee Gregory

Coco Kopelman

Nicole Limbocker

Barbara McLaughlin

Leslie Perkin

Sarah S. Powers

With special thanks to Kelsey Banfield, who coordinated on behalf of The Society.

RECIPE AND ENTERTAINING CONTRIBUTORS

Jessie Araskog

Victoria Amory

Wendy Arriz

Muffie Potter Aston

Kelsey Banfield

Patricia Banfield

Ines Bausili

Patrice Bell

Peggy Bousquette

Alicia Bouzán Cordon

Jane Bowling

Chesie Breen

Ridgely Brode

Tory Burch

Susan Burke

Virginia Burke

Hilary Califano

Catherine Carey

Nancy Coffey

Leslie Coleman

Katie Colgate

Nancy Mulholland Conroy

Patricia Cox

Dianne G. Crary

Jennifer Creel

Mimi Curtis

Mary Darling

Andi Davis

Bambi de la Gueronniere

Hilary Dick

June Dyson

Ruth G. Fleischmann

Libby Fitzgerald

Jean Fitzsimmons

Kelly Forsberg

Annabelle Fowlkes

Elizabeth Fuller

Barbara Gimbel

Sallie Giordano

Anne Grauso

Jamee Gregory

Tom Guinzburg

B. D. Guernsey

Alexia Hamm Ryan

Barbara Harbach

Leslie Heaney

Jimmie Holland, M.D.

Alison Barr Howard

Hedvig Hricak, M.D.

Kelley Johnston

Cindy Kelly

Nicola Kissane

Coco Kopelman

Nicole Limbocker

Suzanne McDonnell Long

Deborah Panaiotopolous

Helena Martinez

Karen May

Barbara McLaughlin

Grace Meigher

Joyce Moss

Eugenie R. Niven

Martha J. O'Brien

Kenneth Offit, M.D.

Dayssi Olarte de Kanavos

Department of Pediatrics

Leslie Perkin

Debra L. Pipines

Ashley D. Potter

Sarah S. Powers

Annette U. Rickel, Ph.D.

Meile Rockefeller

Donna Rosen

Vera Safai

Lisa Selby

Evelyn Angevine Silla

Christina Smith

Tracy Snyder

Emily Sonnenblick, M.D.

Daisy Soros

Leith Rutherford Talamo

Kathy Thomas

Kimberly Tighe

Barbara Tollis

Yolanda Toth

Maria Villalba

Christina Keane Vita

Alexis Waller

Patsy Warner

Amy Whitely

Judith Winslow

Laura Yaggy

Contents

A Note from the Chairman of Memorial Sloan-Kettering Cancer Center

ON BEHALF OF the Board of Overseers and Board of Managers, we are thankful that a portion of the proceeds from *Park Avenue Potluck* will be donated to patient care at Memorial Sloan-Kettering Cancer Center. We also give our heartfelt gratitude to the members of The Society, who have created The Society's first-ever cookbook and hope you will delight in recipes that have warmed the hearths of many devoted friends of the Center.

Memorial Sloan-Kettering's patients and their families have benefited enormously from the generosity, talents, and dedication of Society volunteers. A passion for patient treatment and care motivates this extraordinary organization to achieve excellence in all that they undertake.

I look forward to continued partnership between the Center and The Society. Together we will ensure that MSKCC stays in the forefront of cancer research, patient care, and education.

DOUGLAS A. WARNER III
CHAIRMAN
BOARDS OF OVERSEERS AND MANAGERS

An Introduction to The Society of Memorial Sloan-Kettering Cancer Center

I am delighted to introduce you to The Society of Memorial Sloan-Kettering Cancer Center and our volunteer and fund-raising activities—including *Park Avenue Potluck*—that promote the well-being of patients and their families who come to the Center from all over the world. Founded in 1946 by Clelia Delafield and a small group of women, The Society is dedicated to supporting cancer research and providing public education on the prevention, early detection, and treatment of cancer. The torch is passed to new generations of volunteers and fund-raisers through the Associates, a committee which introduces a younger generation to the work of The Society, and the "Kids Kick In" Committee, which teaches children of Society members the joy of volunteerism from an early age.

As extraordinary advances in science, medicine, and new technologies are introduced, The Society has continually responded to the needs of the Center and its patients through the ambitious work of its fund-raising and volunteer committees. Today, Society members work very closely with the physicians and other MSKCC staff to provide a wealth of programs, services, and patient activities.

Throughout the year, The Society conducts a variety of fund-raising initiatives including high-profile special events such as the Annual Preview Party for the International Fine Art and Antiques Dealer Show and the presentation of the annual Society Awards for Excellence. Through campaigns such as The Society's Annual Appeal, board members solicit support for a particular area of the Center by writing personal letters to friends and relatives; and the Special Projects Committee raises funds for projects that are too early in their development for conventional funding. The Associates concentrate their efforts on fund-raising for the Department of Pediatrics, including the presence of the clowns from The Big Apple Circus Clown

Care Unit®. Funds raised at The Society-operated MSKCC Thrift Shop also support our programs at the Center.

Over the years, proceeds from these events have been used to support innovative basic and clinical research as well as a vast array of programs and initiatives that provide special comforts to patients and their families. Throughout the year, The Society's Fresh Flower Program places fresh flowers in public areas of the hospital, and during the holidays, the hospital is decorated in a splendor that could rival the finest holiday windows in New York City. Patients in isolation have video phones to stay in close touch with their loved ones, and a Sunday Tea is served to patients and their families. Thanks to the "kindness of strangers" and the generosity of members and friends of The Society, these simple gestures—like the fine art that is placed by the Art Committee throughout the hospital—are an important part of the healing in Memorial Hospital.

The publication of *Park Avenue Potluck* represents the wonderful combined talents of the members of The Society, who share a passionate dedication to Memorial Sloan-Kettering's overall mission of providing the best cancer care available anywhere in the world to our patients. We are grateful to Florence Fabricant and Rizzoli Publications for their wisdom and guidance in putting together this collection of family recipes—some of which have been handed down from mothers to daughters. They are truly potluck dishes that we are pleased to bring "from our house to your house." We are also delighted that a recipe from the patients in the Department of Pediatrics is included in this cookbook. Most importantly, the funds raised from this cookbook will support Society programs to offer hope and healing to the patients and their families. I am proud of the legacy of volunteerism and giving that is the heart and soul of The Society.

VERA SAFAI
PRESIDENT
THE SOCIETY OF MEMORIAL SLOAN-KETTERING CANCER CENTER
2005–2007

An Appreciation from the Editor

What impressed me first, when I was initially approached about editing this book, was the dedication and enthusiasm of The Society's members. Then I discovered that these women are not just savvy hosts but also skilled home cooks. I was astonished at the diversity, culinary merit, and inventiveness of the recipes submitted. Most have been handed down over several generations of hostesses. Some have strong ethnic and regional accents. Very few came from chefs or restaurants, but they are all suited for entertaining, with an eye toward advance preparation—casseroles are superb for that—and ease of presentation. Above all, they are dishes that are designed to please guests.

The contributors were extremely generous in permitting me to make changes that I felt were needed to fine-tune their recipes. Most of the revisions had to do with ingredients; many of the heirloom recipes needed a little updating. The results did not diminish the ease with which most of them can be prepared.

Working on this book has expanded my personal repertory of recipes for entertaining. I share, with these women, a love of good food, of being able to greet guests and honor them with a delicious meal prepared with care and served on my own collection of dishes, utensils, and platters, lovingly assembled over the years. I understand the importance, as they do, of candles and fresh flowers. I appreciate, as they do, being able to organize a breezy summer weekend buffet that includes fish from the grill and corn on the cob from a local farm stand, as well as having an elegant dinner party on a chilly night in the city.

I am deeply grateful to The Society for welcoming me, sharing with me, and giving me this opportunity to add my personal tweaks to what they already do so well.

FLORENCE FABRICANT

A Guide for Entertaining

*I*t takes generosity of spirit to entertain well, to see to all the details, and to attend to the comfort of guests. And it is that same generosity that has motivated a group of busy women to devote countless hours to making the day-to-day lives of patients at Memorial Sloan-Kettering, especially children, happier, more colorful, and more diverting than they might be otherwise.

And when these smart, accomplished women find the time to entertain, which they do with astonishing frequency, be it at a small dinner or intimate family gathering, a big buffet or holiday celebration, or a last-minute potluck party, they attend to the details with the enviable ease and the welcoming warmth of practiced hostesses.

With this book, The Society of Memorial Sloan-Kettering Cancer Center is offering you—the reader, the cook, the host and hostess—the ultimate personal potluck: time-tested recipes and ideas for entertaining from their homes to yours.

PLANNING

The first step is to decide what type of party or dinner you will be having and plan all the details that will be appropriate. The best planning results in a party that frees the host or hostess from the kitchen and permits him or her to mingle with the guests.

"A good party takes planning, but once it starts you can relax and enjoy every minute." Jamee Gregory

"The great thing about having parties today is that the host or hostess does not have to prepare the entire meal and can concentrate on just one great dish." Kelly Forsberg

"You must remember to start with an empty dishwasher!" Chesie Breen

INVITATIONS

For a sit-down or buffet dinner, a luncheon or a cocktail party, you have to begin inviting your guests about a month in advance. But then, there are the last-minute, spontaneous parties and gatherings, and sometimes, these are the most enjoyable.

"Our guests are from different worlds, different circles and occupations, and we love to mix them." Donna Rosen

"There are a number of occasions when I think it's fun and appropriate to mix adults and children." Dayssi Olarte de Kanavos

"I call my guests on the phone first and follow up with a printed reminder." Jamee Gregory

MENUS

Organizing the details of the menu is the most important element of the party, regardless of whether you will be doing all the cooking, or will mix prepared foods with homemade, or will engage a caterer. When it comes to the food, the better your planning, the easier and more enjoyable the party will be.

"No matter what, you should plan a party and a menu that will please the men. That's why I'll serve huge chocolate desserts." Leslie Perkin

"I design every menu according to what the men will eat." Chesie Breen

"The menu is determined by the event but more and more I find that the simpler the better. Since I believe that food is love, I tend to choose dishes that are likely to please my guests." Coco Kopelman

"My entertaining has become increasingly informal because my friends come over with their young kids. We do a big pot of chili in the kitchen, or a lasagna." Kelsey Banfield

"I go to several markets that I like and get inspired by what they have that's fresh and looks good." Dayssi Olarte de Kanavos

"I like to figure out the main course first and then plan the first course to balance it, with ingredients that are not the same, not even the same colors." Karen May

"We're always prepared for vegetarians by having enough side dishes." Donna Rosen

"It's a good idea to have a signature dish that people look forward to." Jamee Gregory

COOKING AND PREPARATION

Your guests should not be guinea pigs. As a general rule, plan on serving reliable dishes that you know how to prepare, with ingredients you can easily obtain, to avoid guesswork or last-minute crises. And they should also be dishes that are easily served and conveniently eaten.

"I'm experienced enough by now to know what to put together that is easy, but is very warm and welcoming."
Barbara Tollis

"When you're creative you can do a lot with a little; our recipes are not made with exotic ingredients." Vera Safai

"You learn how to juggle homemade with store-bought and semi-prepared. For a buffet I make sure that the food I serve can be eaten with just a fork, and my hors d'oeuvres are always bite-size so they're easy to eat." Chesie Breen

SETTING THE TABLE

Regardless of whether you are serving in the kitchen, in a formal dining room, on a terrace, or at the beach, the utensils and accessories should be appropriate to the occasion. But mixing and matching is fine, too. Just keep in mind the comfort of your guests when you decide on a table setting. And most of the time, taking that extra step to decant juice into a pitcher or mustard into a little dish makes for a more gracious setting, regardless of the occasion. Similarly, providing cloth napkins is more accommodating than using paper.

"Setting the table is the most fulfilling part of the party preparations." Coco Kopelman

"For a seated dinner you must decide who sits where in advance and it's best to have legible place cards." Virginia Burke

"If your guests do not know each other, write their names on the backs of the place cards, as well as the front, so others at the table can read them too." Florence Fabricant

"I love special occasions like Halloween so I can decorate with tons of pumpkins, brass candlesticks, and trick-or-treat candy." Kim Tighe

"Even when the occasion is informal, I use silver and china. Why own them if you don't use them? And you don't have to be dressed up to eat with a proper fork." Peggy Bousquette

"Paper and plastic are for the children. I think everyone deserves to eat from beautiful things." Anne Grauso

"Flowers are of utmost importance. What could be more beautiful and welcoming than an enormous vase filled to the brim with cherry blossoms, magnolia branches, or peonies? And flickering candles make everything glow." Jamee Gregory

"I use oversize, patterned cloth napkins that are easy to launder." Felicia Blum

"You can serve soup in mugs or espresso cups." Chesie Breen

"I don't plan to serve bread, unless it's a toast garnish of some kind." Leslie Perkin

SERVING

For a seated dinner one option would be for the host or hostess to bring the food out and place bowls and platters on the table or on a sideboard for guests to help themselves. Another would be to hire one or more servers to pass the food and clear the plates or to serve from the buffet. For a larger party, a buffet is the only convenient way to offer the food and either the guests or the waiters can do the serving.

"If we're having ten people or more, we hire help for serving so I don't have to be in the kitchen and can attend to my guests." Peggy Bousquette

"It's great to put the wine right on the table so guests can help themselves. It's more relaxing that way." Karen May

"I always want my guests to feel as if it is a family occasion, like Thanksgiving — everyone is welcome to help." Barbara Tollis

AFTER DINNER

These days fewer and fewer people drink coffee or tea at the end of dinner. But it is considerate to be prepared with tea and coffee — decaffeinated is the usual request — in case someone does want it. And have some artificial sweetener on hand. Even if you do not use it, your guests might prefer it.

"When I serve a frozen dessert at the table, I will opt for demi-tasse in the living room afterwards to use my collection of un-matched cups, brought out on a serving tray." Coco Kopelman

"Serving coffee and after-dinner drinks in the living room and not at the table gives guests a chance to mingle and regroup." Jamee Gregory

THE PARK AVENUE PANTRY

Keeping some staple ingredients on hand in the cupboard, refrigerator, or freezer
will guarantee that you can pull together a party on a moment's notice.

PANTRY SHELF:

Oils, especially extra virgin olive

Vinegars, especially balsamic, red wine,
white wine, sherry

Crackers

Jams and chutneys

Honey, syrups

Flour, sugars, sugar substitute

Sea salt, whole black peppercorns, spices

Tomato products:
puree, whole San Marzano, paste

Chicken broth, bouillon

Pasta, rice, couscous, lentils

Mustard, ketchup, mayonnaise, soy sauce

Canned tuna, anchovies

Dried mushrooms

FREEZER:

Nuts

Phyllo

Vegetables:
baby peas, spinach, artichokes

Raspberries, blueberries

Ice cream, sorbet

Ice

REFRIGERATOR:

Cheeses

Butter

Yogurt, sour cream, crème frâiche

Bacon

Lemons and limes

Tinned foie gras

White wine, champagne, beer

Olives and pickles

MISCELLANEOUS:

Cocktail napkins

Toothpicks

Candles

Sealable plastic bags

Spirits, liquors

Throwing a dinner or lunch party is a spontaneous happening
that stems from a love of people and enjoyment of friends.
For me, entertaining is part of the "living well is the best revenge"
theory of life and gives me an opportunity to share what I do best.
Offering good food and decorating with lovely flowers and pretty
linens are ways of giving my friends happiness.

—NAN KEMPNER

LIBATIONS

San Diego Frozen Margaritas

Pond Water

Sparkling Clear Sangria

Paris Iced Tea

Swedish Christmas Glogg

Left: Sparkling Clear Sangria

KELLY FORSBERG

San Diego Frozen Margaritas

I GREW UP IN SAN DIEGO, A STONE'S THROW FROM THE MEXICAN BORDER. SO MEXICAN FOOD WAS FREQUENTLY ON THE FAMILY MENU, AND ALONG WITH IT, MARGARITAS, OF COURSE! WE CONCOCTED THIS RECIPE TO USE WHEN THE LIME TREE IN OUR BACKYARD WENT ON STRIKE OR WHEN WE DID NOT HAVE TIME TO SQUEEZE A TON OF FRESH LIMES. THE LIMEADE HAS GOOD FLAVOR AND BLENDS BEAUTIFULLY WITH THE ICE FOR A PERFECT SLUSHY CONSISTENCY. THESE ARE PARTY MARGARITAS, SIMPLY PUT. FOR A BIG GROUP, YOU CAN DOUBLE OR TRIPLE THE RECIPE AND LADLE THE COCKTAIL FROM A PUNCH BOWL. USING CHILLED GLASSES HELPS TO MAINTAIN THE QUALITY OF THE DRINK.

3 LIMES

SALT, OPTIONAL

1 12-OUNCE CAN FROZEN LIMEADE

1 1/2 CUPS SILVER OR REPOSADO TEQUILA

1/2 CUP TRIPLE SEC OR COINTREAU

Tequila is made from fermented and distilled agave juice, and any tequila you buy should be labeled 100 percent blue agave, the plant that yields the best juice. Silver or blanco ("white") unaged tequila will give these cocktails a clean, strong jolt. Reposado ("rested") tequila has been aged in wood for a few months. Its flavor is mellower than the silver, but it is also excellent in this cocktail. Do not use añejo ("aged") tequila because it has an inappropriate richness for cocktails. And never buy "gold" tequila, which is always an inexpensive blend and not 100 percent blue agave.

6 SERVINGS

Juice two of the limes and cut the third one in 8 wedges. Use 2 of the wedges to rub the rims of 6 cocktail glasses or old-fashioned glasses. If desired, place salt on a plate and dip the rims in the salt to coat them. Chill the glasses.

Place the limeade, tequila, triple sec, and 3 cups of ice cubes in a blender. Blend until slushy and smooth. Divide among the glasses, over ice in old-fashioned glasses, or straight up in cocktail glasses.

Pond Water

I LOVE TO SERVE MY GUESTS A FUN COCKTAIL AT THE START OF A PARTY.
MY HUSBAND, MARIO, AND I CREATED THIS ONE DURING A LONG HOT SUMMER
IN MILLBROOK, NEW YORK, AT OUR HOUSE, FROG POND. MY SISTERS ALSO
HAD A HAND IN IT. BUT THIS TIME THERE WERE NOT "TOO MANY COOKS, OR BARTENDERS!"
SINCE THE VODKA IS THE BASIS FOR THIS COCKTAIL, DO NOT SKIMP ON QUALITY.
A PREMIUM VODKA IS WHAT YOU SHOULD USE. THIS COCKTAIL WOULD ALSO PLEASE MARTINI
LOVERS—ITS SWEET COMPONENT DOES NOT TAKE OVER. AND WHEN MADE WITH GOOD GIN
INSTEAD OF VODKA, ITS HERBACEOUS FLAVOR IS DELIGHTFULLY INTENSIFIED.

1/3 CUP SUGAR

1 CUP VODKA

1/2 CUP LIMONCELLO LIQUEUR

1/2 CUP LIME JUICE

5 SPRIGS FRESH THYME

4 SLICES LIME

Place the sugar and 1/3 cup water in a saucepan, bring to a simmer, and cook just until the sugar dissolves. Alternatively, combine the sugar and water in a glass measuring cup. Microwave for 1 minute, just until the sugar dissolves. This is simple syrup. Set it aside.

In a large cocktail shaker or a 1-quart canning jar, mix the vodka, limoncello, and lime juice. Pour in the sugar syrup, fill the jar with ice, and shake.

Rub the rims of 4 martini glasses or wine goblets with one of the thyme sprigs. Strain the cocktails into the glasses and serve each garnished with a sprig of thyme and a lime slice.

Martini glasses, or cocktail glasses, are certainly back in style.
And if you regularly serve cocktails, or have guests who might ask
for a martini or a Manhattan, it pays to have some on the bar.
Thrift shops and antique stores are good sources if you prefer your
cocktails to be properly retro. But avoid buying oversize cocktail glasses.
Those holding four ounces might seem a tad skimpy according to
today's standards, so six ounces is fine. Larger than that is excessive
and hard to handle. You can always provide refills.

Sparkling Clear Sangria

*Y*OU USUALLY SEE SANGRIA MADE WITH RED WINE. BUT I PREFER TO USE WHITE WINE BECAUSE IT IS MORE REFRESHING. THIS SANGRIA IS TERRIFIC WITH MEXICAN FOOD. EVEN THOUGH THE WINE IS MIXED WITH FRUIT AND GRAPPA, IT IS IMPORTANT TO CHOOSE A WINE OF DECENT QUALITY, ONE THAT YOU WOULD BE READY TO DRINK ON ITS OWN. BECAUSE OF THE AMOUNT OF CITRUS FRUIT IN THE RECIPE, A FULL-BODIED WINE, LIKE A CHARDONNAY OR VIOGNIER, WOULD WORK BETTER THAN A MORE ACIDIC VARIETY LIKE SAUVIGNON BLANC. IF THE WINE IS RUNNING LOW, I LIKE TO ADD SOME SELTZER AND EXTRA LEMON TO STRETCH IT.

2 ORANGES, CHILLED AND SLICED THIN

2 LIMES, CHILLED AND SLICED THIN

2 LEMONS, CHILLED AND SLICED THIN

1 1/2 LITERS (2 BOTTLES OR 1 MAGNUM) DRY WHITE WINE, CHILLED

1/2 CUP GRAPPA OR BRANDY, CHILLED

Place all the fruit in a clear glass pitcher. Use a big wooden spoon to lightly muddle the fruit and release some of the juice. Add the wine and the grappa (or brandy). Chill for at least 30 minutes before serving.

If you prefer to make a red wine sangria, substitute ripe peaches, peeled, pitted and sliced, for the limes, and be sure to use brandy in place of the grappa.

8 SERVINGS

Not only are a clear glass pitcher and a wooden spoon the classic
utensils for serving sangria, but also a long skewer, with which you
can spear the fruit and distribute it among the glasses, is useful.
Though it is best to prepare the sangria with chilled ingredients so
it can be served without ice, there is nothing wrong with pouring it
over ice in wine goblets.

Paris Iced Tea

WE discovered this refreshing tea during one hot summer day in Paris, and we enjoyed it on the patio of our hotel. My husband is in the fashion business, which takes us to Paris for weeks at a time, even in mid-summer. We did our best to make this recipe as close to the Parisian version as possible. It continues to be a favorite at all my summer gatherings, bringing that taste of Paris home.

Iced tea is best served in tall, narrow glasses. And if you are a shopper at antiques fairs, you might even find silver sippers to go with them.

1 cup sugar

Juice of 2 limes

3 orange spice tea bags or 1 tablespoon loose orange spice tea

1/2 pint fresh raspberries

1 cup fresh blueberries

2 limes, in 12 wedges

12 servings

Place the sugar in a saucepan, add 1 cup of water, bring to a simmer, and cook just until the sugar dissolves. Alternatively, combine the sugar and water in a glass measuring cup and microwave for 1 minute, until the sugar dissolves. Add the lime juice. Transfer to a metal bowl and place in a larger bowl filled with ice and water to chill.

Place the tea bags, or loose tea in a tea infuser, in a pitcher. Add 2 quarts of water that has boiled and then cooled for 2 minutes. Steep for about 10 minutes. Remove the tea. Refrigerate until ready to serve.

To serve, divide the raspberries and blueberries among 12 tall glasses. Add the ice and tea. Garnish with a lime wedge. Pour the syrup into a small pitcher and serve it alongside for sweetening the tea to taste. If you toss the berries in a little of the sugar syrup, you may find that your guests will prefer less additional sweetening.

Though the recipe calls for orange spice tea, almost any kind of tea can be used. Jasmine tea, with its lovely perfume, would be a fine choice, as would Earl Grey, which is seasoned with bergamot, an orangelike citrus fruit. Another option, especially if you will be pouring the tea from a glass pitcher, is to use a flower tea. Flower teas are tightly wrapped balls of tea leaves that open up like a flower in hot water and produce a mild, elegant brew. The eye-appeal is undeniable. It really pays to use whole-leaf loose tea for all your tea-making. There are holders of all kinds on the market that can contain loose tea for brewing. But if you prefer to use tea bags, buy only those with whole-leaf tea.

Swedish Christmas Glogg

At Christmas, my in-laws, the Forsbergs, would always have a traditional Swedish celebration. A big black pot of glogg would be warming on the stove, and as guests arrived they would be served a cup of it. It smells really delicious when it is heating. But it is also very strong, so serve small portions. A little goes a long way.

A punch bowl is a very particular item of limited use. Punch bowls, ladles, and cups can be rented. Alternatively, with a certain amount of creativity, a substitute can be found. A big, deep casserole is one option. A generous soup tureen is another.

10 whole cloves

12 whole cardamom pods

1 stick cinnamon

3 liters dry red wine (4 bottles or 2 magnums)

Peel of 1 orange

1 cup white, Demerara, or turbinado sugar

1 cup raisins

1½ cups aquavit

2 cups blanched almonds

12 to 15 servings

Place the cloves, cardamom, and cinnamon in a piece of cheesecloth and tie securely. Place the wine in a large stainless steel or enameled cast-iron pot on the stove. Add the spices, orange peel, and sugar.

Heat the wine until it is barely simmering and stir until the sugar dissolves. Do not allow it to boil. Transfer the mixture to a pitcher or bowl, cover, and let it sit for at least 6 hours, preferably overnight.

Place the raisins in a bowl, add the aquavit, cover, and set aside.

Shortly before serving, remove the spice bag and orange peel from the wine. Drain the aquavit from the raisins and add it. Place the raisins in a small bowl.

Warm the glogg again. Pour it from a pitcher into punch cups with a few raisins and almonds added to each serving. Alternatively, if you are using a punch bowl, you can add the raisins and almonds to the bowl, so guests can ladle the raisins and almonds into their cups themselves.

A rich, hearty, young red works best for glogg. Look for a California Merlot or Syrah, or a Montepulciano d'Abruzzo from Italy. As for the aquavit, you do not need a fancy one either. But do be sure your whole spices are fresh, for ultimate fragrance and flavor. If necessary, buy a new supply for this recipe. The glogg will have a richer taste if it is made with light brown turbinado or Demerara sugar instead of white sugar. Both of these natural brown sugars—they are not made with molasses like regular brown sugar—are widely available.

SMALL BITES

Indulgent Spiced Pecans

Old-School Tomato Sandwiches

Asian Ratatouille Spread

Pub-Style Cheddar Chutney Croustades

Bruschetta with Pears and Blue Cheese

Parmesan Crackers

Rainbow Goat Cheese Terrine

Maryland Crabmeat Spread

Scallop Puffs for a Crowd

Warm Spinach and Boursin Cheese Dip

Cheese Tart from Italy

Spanakopita

Left to right: Scallop Puffs for a Crowd, Asian Ratatouille Spread, and Parmesan Crackers

Indulgent Spiced Pecans

I WAS TEMPTED TO MAKE THESE AFTER SEEING A SIMILAR RECIPE IN A FOOD MAGAZINE. PECANS ARE THE ONLY NUT I'LL BREAK A DIET FOR. THESE COCKTAIL NIBBLES CAN BE VERY SPICY, SO I HAVE REDUCED THE AMOUNT OF CAYENNE TO ALLOW THE OTHER FLAVORS, LIKE SOY AND ONION, TO COME THROUGH. THEY'RE THE PROVERBIAL ADDICTIVE SNACK—YOU CAN'T EAT JUST ONE. GUESTS REALLY LOVE THEM. AND IF YOU HAVE MADE THEM IN ADVANCE AND STORED THEM IN AN AIRTIGHT CONTAINER, YOU CAN GIVE THEM A QUICK REFRESHER IN A MICROWAVE OVEN. CONSIDER PUTTING SMALL BOWLS OF THESE PECANS ON THE TABLE WHEN YOU SERVE A SIMPLE GREEN SALAD. GUESTS WILL LOVE TO NIBBLE THE NUTS ALONG WITH THE GREENS.

3 TABLESPOONS CHOPPED ONIONS

2 TABLESPOONS UNSALTED BUTTER, MELTED

1 1/2 CUPS PECAN HALVES

1 TABLESPOON SOY SAUCE

1/4 TEASPOON CAYENNE, OR TO TASTE

SALT, OPTIONAL

Regular brand-name supermarket soy sauce is the lowest common denominator. The best all-around soy sauce for culinary and table use is either Japanese tamari, which is a rich, often organic sauce, or Chinese light soy. The "light" in this case has nothing to do with salt or calories—it designates the texture. In fact, Chinese light soy, which is inexpensive if you buy it in Chinatown, is actually saltier than Chinese dark soy.

4 TO 6 SERVINGS

Preheat the oven to 300 degrees. Line a jelly-roll pan with foil.

Squeeze the onion in a garlic press into a bowl. Stir in the onion pulp from the press. Add the melted butter and pecans. Add the remaining ingredients and toss to combine.

Spread the pecans in the pan in a single layer and bake about 20 minutes, gently turning the pecans from time to time.

Transfer the pecans to several thicknesses of paper towel to drain briefly. If desired, toss with salt and more cayenne. Store in an airtight container until ready to serve.

NOTE: Pecans have a higher fat content than any other nut. As a result, they can quickly go rancid or stale. It is best to buy fresh, high-quality pecan halves for this recipe and store them in the freezer until you use them.

Old-School Tomato Sandwiches

*I*N MY HOUSE IN SUMMER, WE PROBABLY EAT MORE FRESH, RIPE TOMATOES WITH MAYONNAISE ON WHITE BREAD THAN ANYTHING ELSE. CUT IN SMALL SQUARES OR TRIANGLES, THEY BECOME DELICIOUS HORS D'OEUVRES WITH DRINKS. THEY ARE THE ULTIMATE ANTIDOTE TO ELABORATE, SHOW-STOPPING HORS D'OEUVRES AND ARE EASY ON THE HOST AND THE GUESTS. THESE SANDWICHES ARE JUST A STEP REMOVED FROM A B.L.T., A STANDARD FAMILY LUNCH.

WHEN GUESTS ARE EXPECTED, ADD SOME LOBSTER OR SHRIMP AND MAKE THE SANDWICHES ON AN EGG-BASED BREAD, LIKE A BRIOCHE LOAF: IT WILL TURN THE SANDWICHES INTO LUXURY GOODS. HOMEMADE MAYONNAISE IS ALWAYS WELCOME FOR THIS RECIPE, ESPECIALLY IF IT IS NOT RUNNY, BUT THE REGULAR SUPERMARKET KIND IS PERFECTLY ACCEPTABLE. FOR AN EXTRA TOUCH, FOLD SOME MINCED BASIL OR A DOLLOP OF PESTO INTO THE MAYONNAISE.

IF YOU PUT OUT A PLATTER OF THE SANDWICHES, YOU CAN PILE SEVERAL LAYERS ON A LARGE SERVING DISH. BUT IF THEY ARE TO BE PASSED, IT IS BEST TO USE A SMALLER PLATE AND A SINGLE, SLIGHTLY OVERLAPPING LAYER THAT CAN BE REPLENISHED.

8 TO 12 SERVINGS

1 LOAF GOOD-QUALITY THIN-SLICED SANDWICH BREAD, 1 POUND

5 TABLESPOONS MAYONNAISE

3 RIPE BEEFSTEAK OR HEIRLOOM TOMATOES, PEELED
(SEE SIDEBAR, BELOW)

FRESH BASIL SPRIGS, FOR GARNISH

Discard the end slices of the loaf. Trim the crusts from the bread. Arrange 8 slices on a work surface and spread each with 1 teaspoon mayonnaise.

Remove cores from the tomatoes and slice the tomatoes fairly thin. Arrange the slices on the bread. Spread remaining bread with remaining mayonnaise and cover sandwiches.

Cut each sandwich in four on the diagonal, to make 32 triangles. Arrange them on a platter, cover, and refrigerate until 30 minutes before serving. Remove from refrigerator, garnish the platter with basil sprigs, and pass, with cocktails.

Peeling the tomatoes is an elegant touch for guests. You can forego this step for family. But there is an alternative to the method of peeling tomatoes by dipping them in boiling water for 30 seconds: a new, serrated peeler for tomatoes and soft fruits is now available at housewares stores.

Asian Ratatouille Spread

THIS RECIPE FROM MY SISTER IS A QUICK, TASTY, AND CROWD-PLEASING HORS D'OEUVRE. MY BOYFRIEND CALLS IT A "PARTY IN YOUR MOUTH." THE BASIS FOR IT IS GRILLED OR ROASTED VEGETABLES. YOU CAN EITHER DO THEM YOURSELF OR, FOR THE EASIEST SOLUTION, BUY THEM IN A GOOD PREPARED-FOOD SHOP. WITH PURCHASED VEGETABLES, THE WHOLE THING TAKES ABOUT FIVE MINUTES, START TO FINISH. I ESPECIALLY LIKE TO USE RED AND YELLOW PEPPERS, CARROTS, YELLOW SQUASH, ZUCCHINI, EGGPLANT, AND FENNEL. AN ONION-AND-MUSHROOM MIX WITH OR WITHOUT SOME OF THE OTHER VEGETABLES, IS ALSO WORTH CONSIDERING. OR THE SPREAD COULD BE MADE MONOCHROMATICALLY, USING JUST PEPPERS OR EGGPLANT. AND BY ALL MEANS, USE WASABI RICE CRACKERS. THAT'S WHERE THE "PARTY IN YOUR MOUTH" COMES IN. OF COURSE, IF YOU ARE PUT OFF BY SPICES, PLAIN RICE CRACKERS WOULD BE FINE, TOO.

8 SERVINGS

1 CLOVE GARLIC

1 SLICE PEELED GINGER ABOUT ¼-INCH THICK, CHOPPED

1 POUND MIXED GRILLED VEGETABLES, HOMEMADE OR PURCHASED, CHOPPED

2 TABLESPOONS WHITE MISO PASTE

4 TABLESPOONS SOY SAUCE

2 TEASPOONS ASIAN TOASTED SESAME OIL

2 PACKAGES RICE CRACKERS, WASABI OR PLAIN

Turn on a food processor. With the machine running, drop the garlic and ginger into the feed tube to mince them. Turn off the machine, scrape down the sides, and place the grilled vegetables in the work bowl. Mix the miso paste, soy sauce, and sesame oil together in a dish and add to the vegetables. Pulse the mixture until the vegetables are very finely chopped. Do not puree them. You may have to stop the machine once or twice to mix the vegetables and scrape down the sides of the container so the chopping will be uniform.

Transfer the mixture to a dish or mound it on a plate and surround it with the crackers for serving. Alternatively, you can spread the mixture on the crackers and pass them on a tray.

Though a bottled Chinese or Japanese seasoning sauce like ponzu can be used, making the soy-based mixture from scratch is no challenge. These days, most health-food stores carry miso paste. There are several kinds—white, yellow, and red—ranging from mild to strong. You will have leftovers after you have made this recipe, but the paste will keep for months in the refrigerator. Add it to stir-fries and stews, even those that are not particularly Asian, to thicken the sauce and punch up the flavor: miso is a worthwhile addition that is destined to become more popular, and perhaps even to become a pantry staple. The deliciously warming miso soup often served in Japanese restaurants consists mainly of miso paste dissolved in stock. Miso paste could even become a secret ingredient in your chicken soup!

Pub-Style Cheddar Chutney Croustades

THIS RECIPE IS A REAL HAND-ME-DOWN. MY FRIEND, MIA BUHL, GOT IT FROM A FRIEND OF HERS, AND THEN GAVE IT TO ME. THE CROUSTADES ARE SCRUMPTIOUS TIDBITS THAT ARE TANGY, RICH, AND A LITTLE OUT OF THE ORDINARY, THOUGH CHEDDAR AND CHUTNEY MAKE FOR A STANDARD ENGLISH PUB-STYLE SANDWICH WITH A PINT OF ALE. BUT THESE CAN EASILY ACCOMPANY A GLASS OF CHARDONNAY. I ESPECIALLY LIKE TO SERVE THEM IN AUTUMN.

1 JAR (10 OUNCES) MAJOR GREY'S MANGO CHUTNEY
1/2 CUP GRATED SHARP CHEDDAR CHEESE
24 THIN SLICES BAGUETTE, LIGHTLY TOASTED
2 TABLESPOONS MINCED MINT OR CILANTRO LEAVES

Preheat the oven to 350 degrees. Line a baking sheet with foil.

Puree the chutney in a food processor until smooth. Mix it with the cheese in a bowl. Spoon the mixture onto the toasts and arrange them on the baking sheet.

Bake about 5 minutes, just until warmed through. Arrange on a tray and garnish each with a little mint or cilantro. Serve the croustades as soon as they come out of the oven.

6 SERVINGS

Major Grey's, a type of sweet mango chutney, is probably the most popular
kind of chutney sold outside India. And though it is the first choice for these
hors d'oeuvres, other chutneys, including onion or tomato, can be used
instead. In fact, you might consider making the croustades using two or three
kinds of chutney and serving them at the same time. It may be more work,
but the results are fun to serve. Similarly, you can vary the cheese and use
Gruyère, aged Jack, or Parmesan.

PATRICIA BANFIELD

Bruschetta with Pears and Blue Cheese

THE RECIPE IS SOMETHING WE CONCOCTED FOR THE HOLIDAY SEASON. IT SEEMS THAT OUR GENEROUS FRIENDS AND CLIENTS OFTEN SEND US BASKETS OF WONDERFUL, LUSCIOUS, PLUMP PEARS AS HOLIDAY GIFTS. SINCE THE FRUIT IS RIPE AND ONLY LASTS FOR TEN DAYS AT THE MOST, WE BEGAN INCORPORATING THE PEARS INTO OUR REPERTOIRE OF HORS D'OEUVRES FOR HOLIDAY PARTIES. IT'S NOW BECOME A TRADITION, AND OUR FRIENDS AND FAMILY LOOK FORWARD TO THESE CANAPÉS AT COCKTAIL TIME.

BRUSCHETTA WITH PEARS IS ALSO EXCELLENT ALONGSIDE A SIMPLE FIRST-COURSE SALAD, AND AT THE END OF A MEAL, IT CAN STAND IN FOR A FORMAL CHEESE COURSE. CONSIDER USING TWO DIFFERENT KINDS OF CHEESE, LIKE A SOFT GOAT CHEESE OR AN ITALIAN FONTINA, ALONG WITH THE BLUE CHEESE. AND INSTEAD OF BRUSHING THE BREAD WITH OLIVE OIL, APPLY A SHEER SLICK OF CHUTNEY OR TART QUINCE JAM.

I LONG, THIN FRENCH BAGUETTE, ABOUT 9 OUNCES

2 TABLESPOONS EXTRA VIRGIN OLIVE OIL

3 TABLESPOONS UNSALTED BUTTER

6 JUST-RIPE PEARS, PEELED, CORED, AND THINLY SLICED

6 OUNCES BLUE CHEESE, CRUMBLED

I2 SERVINGS

Preheat the oven to 400 degrees. Line a baking sheet with foil.

Cut the baguette into slices ¼ inch thick. Brush each slice with olive oil and arrange on the baking sheet. Bake for 5 minutes or until lightly toasted. Remove and set aside. Preheat the broiler.

Melt the butter in a large skillet. Add the pear slices and sauté until soft but not mushy. Top each piece of baguette with a pear slice and put some of the blue cheese on top.

Return the bruschettas to the oven and bake for a minute or two, until the cheese starts to melt. Serve warm.

When buying pears, the best way to test them for ripeness is to apply a little pressure at the stem end. The pear should yield slightly. This is a better test than squeezing the larger end because pears ripen from the inside out and by the time the meaty bottom part of the fruit is soft, the pear will be overripe.

Parmesan Crackers

I LOVE THIS RECIPE BECAUSE I CAN MAKE THE DOUGH AHEAD OF TIME AND EVEN BAKE THE CRACKERS UP TO A DAY IN ADVANCE, SO THERE IS NO LAST-MINUTE RUSH. THESE ARE MORE LIKE COOKIES—SHORTBREAD COOKIES WITH CHEESE— THAN THEY ARE LIKE CRACKERS. THE DOUGH CAN BE MIXED IN A FOOD PROCESSOR, THEN FORMED INTO A LOG AND SLICED. THE CRACKERS HARDLY BROWN AND BARELY EXPAND IN THE OVEN IN THE FIRST BAKING. RETURNING THEM TO A HOTTER OVEN GIVES THEM A NICE BURNISH. I SERVE THEM, JUST AS THEY ARE, WITH COCKTAILS, OR ALONGSIDE A SALAD. THEY ARE ASSERTIVELY FLAVORED, SO YOU HAVE TO BE CAREFUL NOT TO SERVE THEM WITH SOMETHING THAT THEY MIGHT OVERPOWER.

1/4 POUND (1 STICK) UNSALTED BUTTER, SOFTENED
PLUS EXTRA FOR GREASING IF NECESSARY
1 CUP FLOUR
1 CUP GRATED PARMIGIANO-REGGIANO, ABOUT 4 OUNCES
FRESHLY GROUND BLACK PEPPER, TO TASTE

8 SERVINGS, ABOUT 40 CRACKERS

Place the butter, flour, cheese, and pepper in a food processor and pulse just until the dough comes together. Divide the dough in half. Turn each half out onto a piece of plastic wrap and form into a log about 1½ inches in diameter. Wrap well and chill until firm, at least 2 hours.

Preheat the oven to 325 degrees.

Lightly grease two baking sheets with butter or line the sheets with parchment. Slice each log into rounds ¼ inch thick and place them an inch apart on the baking sheets. Bake about 12 to 13 minutes, just until firm. You can bake both sheets at the same time, either side by side if your oven is large enough, or on two racks (the middle and upper). But if you do, be sure to reverse the sheets halfway through the baking. They can also be baked one after the other.

Increase the heat to 500 degrees. Return the sheets to the oven, either together on the same rack or one after the other, and bake for about 3 minutes longer, or until the crackers are deeply golden brown all over. Remove from the oven and transfer crackers to a wire rack to cool completely. Serve on a tray or piled in a bowl or small, lined basket.

When shopping for parmesan cheese, always look for genuine Parmigiano-Reggiano from Italy. The name of the cheese must be stamped on the rind. Other countries, including the United States and Argentina, also produce parmesan cheese but they are not as deeply flavored as the Italian import. Buy the cheese fresh, never pre-grated in a container. The best substitute for Parmigiano-Reggiano is Grana Padano, a similar cheese made in the same region.

KELLEY JOHNSTON

Rainbow Goat Cheese Terrine

Knowing I am a fool for goat cheese, my sister gave me this recipe, and it has served me well. I make it frequently for parties, as it is best done ahead of time and kept refrigerated. The recipe can also easily be doubled or tripled and placed on a buffet for a large party. The terrine looks much more complicated than it really is, so guests are bound to be impressed. There is nothing better for a hostess than to wow the party without breaking a sweat. Or, as in this case, barely lighting the stove. You can use interesting molds as well, like heart-shaped or stars, for different occasions.

2 tablespoons slivered almonds or pine nuts, toasted

2 cloves garlic, peeled

12 ounces cream cheese

1 package (5 to 6 ounces) soft goat cheese

1¼ teaspoon dried oregano

Pinch of freshly ground black pepper

¼ cup commercial or homemade pesto (see recipe, pages 88–89)

½ cup sun-dried tomatoes in oil, well-drained and finely chopped

Crackers, toast, bread, or endive leaves for spreading

10 SERVINGS

Lightly toast the nuts in a dry skillet over medium heat, turning them, or in a toaster oven.

Line a 3-cup round bowl, loaf pan, or other mold with plastic wrap.

Turn on a food processor fitted with the regular blade. Drop the garlic down through the feed tube to mince it. Stop the processor and scrape down the sides of the work bowl. Add the cream cheese, goat cheese, oregano, and pepper to the food processor and blend until the mixture is smooth.

Spoon one-third of the cheese mixture into the mold. Spread the pesto over it. Add another third of the cheese and then a layer of the sun-dried tomatoes, followed by the rest of the cheese. Cover and refrigerate at least 3 hours.

To serve, unmold the mixture onto a serving dish and peel off the plastic. Sprinkle the nuts on top and serve with crackers, toast, slices of baguette, or endive leaves for spreading.

NOTE: Tomato pesto from a jar, an item that is frequently sold in fancy food shops, can be substituted for the sun-dried tomatoes. An alternative option is to replace the tomato layer with a thicker one of very finely minced smoked salmon, making for an excellent brunch dish. Make the terrine in a 4-cup mold, with about 6 ounces of salmon. With the salmon, use drained capers or grated lemon zest to decorate the top in place of the nuts, and serve the terrine with bagel chips.

This terrine can be rustic or elegant, depending on how you choose to present it. Unmold it onto a pottery plate with enough of a rim to hold the toast or crackers, and it is as casual as can be. The toast or crackers could even be piled into a basket alongside. But then, there is also the possibility of unmolding the terrine onto fine porcelain, crystal, or glass, carefully arranging the toasts or crackers around it, and placing a silver spreader alongside. That way, it becomes a worthy partner for crystal flutes of Champagne or, with the smoked salmon, brightly fizzy mimosas.

Maryland Crabmeat Spread

THIS IS A DISH THAT A FRIEND OF MINE SERVED WITH COCKTAILS, AND I HAVE FOUND IT TO BE VERY POPULAR. MY FRIEND MADE IT WITH CANNED CRABMEAT BECAUSE SHE COULD NOT GET FRESH, BUT I USE MARYLAND LUMP CRABMEAT. AND I DOUBLE THE RECIPE BECAUSE IT OFTEN GETS SCOOPED UP FAST BY MY GUESTS. I SOMETIMES SERVE IT AS A FIRST COURSE, ON A BED OF BIBB LETTUCE WITH HALVED PEAR TOMATOES AS A GARNISH. THE MIXTURE ALSO MAKES AN EXCELLENT SEAFOOD STUFFING FOR AVOCADO HALVES OR TOMATOES, AS A FIRST COURSE.

6 ounces lump crabmeat

2 tablespoons chopped flat-leaf parsley leaves

1 tablespoon finely chopped onion

¼ cup mayonnaise

1 teaspoon lemon juice

1½ tablespoons cocktail sauce

Crackers or toast rounds, for serving

Drained capers or diced black olives for garnish, optional

Pick over the crabmeat to remove any stray bits of cartilage and place it in a food processor. Add the parsley and onion and pulse briefly to make a finely minced mixture. Transfer it to a bowl and mix in the mayonnaise, lemon juice, and cocktail sauce.

Pile the mixture in a serving dish and refrigerate it until ready to serve with crackers or small toast rounds for spreading. Alternatively, the mixture can be spread on toast or crackers as canapés, each garnished with a caper or piece of olive.

NOTE: Since the crabmeat is finely minced for the recipe, it is not necessary to buy the most expensive jumbo lump variety.

Like the other spreads in this book, all easy staples of the entertaining repertory, this one can be used to make canapés (see the Asian Ratatouille Spread, pages 44–45) or as a filling for fancy tea sandwiches on white bread. Dollops of the crabmeat mixture can also be placed at the base of endive leaves to be passed as hors d'oeuvres. That way you will stretch the number of servings to 12 or more.

Scallop Puffs for a Crowd

I ALWAYS SERVE THESE AT COCKTAIL PARTIES. THEY ARE SIMPLY DIVINE. I LIKE TO GIVE THIS RECIPE TO MY CATERER TO MAKE WHEN I ENTERTAIN CROWDS. MY ONLY PROBLEM IS THAT MY GUESTS LOVE THEM SO MUCH, THEY EAT TOO MANY OF THEM AND THERE ARE NONE LEFT FOR ME!

THOUGH THE RECIPE CALLS FOR TINY, BITE-SIZE MORSELS OF THIS DELECTABLE HORS D'OEUVRE, YOU CAN MAKE LARGER CANAPÉS, OR EVEN USE THE SCALLOP MIXTURE FOR OPEN-FACE SANDWICHES TO SERVE FOR LUNCH WITH SOUP. THE SCALLOP MIXTURE CAN ALSO BE SPOONED INTO SHALLOW RAMEKINS OR EVEN SHELLS, EITHER GENUINE OR PORCELAIN, AND THEN QUICKLY BROILED AND SERVED AS A FIRST COURSE.

3 TABLESPOONS UNSALTED BUTTER

1 POUND SEA SCALLOPS, DICED

2 TEASPOONS FINELY GRATED LEMON ZEST

3 CLOVES GARLIC, MINCED

3 TABLESPOONS CHOPPED FRESH DILL

2 CUPS GRATED GRUYÈRE CHEESE, ABOUT 1/2 POUND

2 1/4 CUPS MAYONNAISE

FRESHLY GROUND WHITE PEPPER, TO TASTE

1 LOAF GOOD-QUALITY THIN-SLICED SANDWICH BREAD

SWEET HUNGARIAN PAPRIKA, FOR DUSTING

18 TO 24 SERVINGS

Melt the butter in a medium skillet or sauté pan over medium-high heat. Add the scallops, lemon zest, and garlic. Cook, stirring constantly, about 2 to 3 minutes, until the scallops are just barely cooked through. Add the dill and cook 30 seconds longer. Transfer the mixture to a bowl and let it cool to room temperature.

Add the cheese, mayonnaise, and pepper to the scallop mixture and stir to combine well.

Preheat a broiler. Line a baking sheet with foil. Trim the crusts from the bread and toast slices under the broiler, turning once, until barely browned. Watch carefully. Cut each slice in 6 squares. You should have 96 small pieces.

Cover each piece of the toast with the scallop mixture and place ½ inch apart on the baking sheet. Dust lightly with paprika. Broil the canapés 5 inches from the heat until puffed and golden, 2 to 3 minutes. Transfer the puffs to platters and serve hot.

NOTE: Try to find genuine Hungarian paprika, which will have a more robust flavor than the kinds sold in typical supermarket spice racks.

Of the various kinds of scallops on the market, sea scallops are best for this recipe. Good Nantucket or Peconic bay scallops are twice the price of sea scallops. Tiny so-called "bay scallops," or calicos, have been frozen and thawed, are tasteless, and are not worth buying. You will notice on the side of a sea scallop, there is a small, rubbery extra piece of meat. Remove and discard this little nugget of tendon the way the chefs do. It does not add anything to your dish.

Warm Spinach and Boursin Cheese Dip

I FIRST TASTED THIS INCREDIBLE DIP AT THE HOME OF FRIENDS IN HOBE SOUND, FLORIDA. IT WAS MADE BY THEIR CHEF, AND HE GAVE ME THE RECIPE.

THE DIP WORKS JUST FINE PLACED ON A COCKTAIL TABLE AND SERVED WARM, WITH CHIPS, BUT THERE ARE OTHER OPTIONS THAT GO BEYOND THE COCKTAIL HOUR. FOR EXAMPLE, THE MIXTURE DOES VERY NICELY AS A TOPPING FOR BAKED FILLETS OF FISH, INCLUDING HALIBUT, FLOUNDER, AND SALMON. IT CAN ALSO BE USED TO STUFF CHICKEN BREASTS, TO FOLD INTO A PLAIN RISOTTO, OR TO TOP BAKED POTATOES THAT HAVE BEEN HALVED, MASHED, PUT BACK INTO THEIR SKINS, AND REHEATED.

CERAMIC OR POTTERY BAKING DISHES IN VARIOUS SIZES, SHALLOW OR DEEP, AND ROUND, SQUARE, OBLONG, OR OVAL ARE INDISPENSABLE FOR ENTERTAINING. THEY COST ONLY A LITTLE MORE THAN GARDEN-VARIETY GLASS ONES FROM THE HARDWARE STORE, BUT MAKE THE PRESENTATION OF DISHES LIKE THE SPINACH AND BOURSIN DIP MORE ATTRACTIVE.

10 OUNCES FRESH SPINACH, STEMS REMOVED

4 PACKAGES PLAIN BOURSIN CHEESE, OR SOFT GOAT CHEESE,
AT ROOM TEMPERATURE, ABOUT 16 OUNCES

SALT AND FRESHLY GROUND BLACK PEPPER, TO TASTE

PINCH OF CAYENNE

1 TABLESPOON EXTRA VIRGIN OLIVE OIL

1/4 CUP FRESHLY GRATED PARMIGIANO-REGGIANO

CHIPS FOR SERVING

12 SERVINGS

Wash the spinach and shake off the excess water. Place in a skillet and cook over medium heat just until the spinach wilts. Wrap the spinach in several thicknesses of paper towel and squeeze out the moisture. Alternatively, you can place the spinach in a potato ricer and press it to squeeze out the moisture. Place the spinach in a food processor and pulse just enough to chop it.

Transfer the spinach to a bowl, add the Boursin, and mix thoroughly. Season to taste with salt, pepper, and cayenne.

About 45 minutes before serving time, preheat the oven to 350 degrees. Use the oil to grease a 9-inch ceramic quiche dish.

Spread the spinach mixture in the dish and sprinkle the Parmigiano-Reggiano on top. Place in the oven and bake about 25 minutes, until the mixture is hot and the top has started to brown.

Serve immediately, with chips for dipping.

The mixture can be spread on thirty-six little toast rounds and placed under the broiler for a few minutes, until lightly browned, and then served as canapés. Made a trifle larger, the canapés are an excellent accompaniment to a first-course soup or a salad. Another possibility, as an hors d'oeuvre, is to use the dip as a stuffing for large cherry tomatoes. Remove any stems from the tomatoes and place them stem-end down on the pan (this keeps them more stable and prevents them from wobbling or tipping over). Cut off the top third from the rounded end and scoop out the insides. Fill the tomatoes with the cheese and spinach mixture and then broil them.

BARBARA MCLAUGHLIN

Cheese Tart from Italy

I WAS GIVEN THIS RECIPE BY A FRIEND OF MINE WHO LEARNED IT WHILE VISITING FRIENDS IN ITALY. IT IS GREAT FOR USING UP BITS OF CHEESE THAT MAY BE ACCUMULATING IN YOUR FRIDGE. THE TART PUFFS DRAMATICALLY AND IS BEST SERVED THE MOMENT IT COMES OUT OF THE OVEN. PUT THE PIE PLATE ON A DINNER PLATE AND BRING IT OUT WITH A SHARP KNIFE AND A PIE SERVER.

1 SHEET PACKAGED PUFF PASTRY

2 CUPS GRATED CHEESE, PREFERABLY A MIXTURE OF GRUYÈRE, PARMESAN, AND PECORINO, ABOUT 1/2 POUND

1/4 CUP HALF-AND-HALF

1 LARGE EGG, LIGHTLY BEATEN

6 TO 8 SERVINGS

Preheat the oven to 350 degrees.

Place the sheet of pastry on a work surface and place an 8-inch or 9-inch glass pie plate on it upside down. Use a sharp knife to trace a circle around the pastry with the pie plate as a guide, discarding the excess from the corners. Turn the pie plate over and fit the round of pastry in it.

Use a fork to mix the cheeses with the half-and-half and the egg until well blended. Spread the cheese mixture over the pastry. Place in the oven and bake about 35 minutes, until the pastry is puffed and browned around the edges.

Serve at once, cutting the cheese tart in wedges.

NOTE: Wedges of this cheese tart may be served alongside a salad, or even as a cheese course after the main course. Some chutney, an onion jam, or sweet-and-sour Italian preserved fruits in mustard (mostarda) make fine accompaniments. It is also excellent when lightly drizzled with saba, a thick, somewhat sweet Italian preparation made from concentrated grapes that is sold in fancy food shops.

Packaged frozen puff pastry sheets are a welcome shortcut for the cook. But there are differences. The brand that is widely sold in supermarkets is missing the one ingredient that makes puff pastry wonderful: butter. Instead, it is produced with a mixture of fats, including trans fats. No legislators have gotten on the bandwagon to free packaged puff pastry of trans fats, nor is it likely to happen. Fortunately, there are brands, which are harder to find but are sold in fancy food shops and online, that are made with butter. Dufour Pastry Kitchens (www.dufourpastrykitchens.com) is one of them.

Spanakopita

THIS recipe came from my Greek grandmother, who was a wonderful cook. I have such fond memories of her food, so it's especially appealing to me to serve her specialties, continuing a family tradition. I like to dress up a platter of spanakopita with a nice herbal garnish, like a feathery bunch of fresh dill. And instead of serving these triangles as an appetizer, a platter of them can go on a buffet with other Greek dishes, including assorted olives, an eggplant dip, thick yogurt seasoned with garlic and dill, a cucumber salad, stuffed grape leaves, and taramosalata dip, all of which can be purchased freshly made or in jars, at fancy food shops. This array would make a perfect prelude to a dinner of Baked Halibut Jardinière (see recipe, pages 136–37) or Moussaka (see recipe, pages 122–23).

3 packages (10 ounces each) frozen chopped spinach

¼ cup extra virgin olive oil

1 bunch scallions, trimmed, with some green left on, chopped

¼ cup finely chopped flat-leaf parsley leaves

½ cup chopped fresh dill

5 large eggs, beaten

2½ cups coarsely crumbled feta cheese, preferably Greek,
about 8 ounces

Salt and freshly ground black pepper, to taste

1 pound phyllo pastry, thawed

¼ pound (1 stick) unsalted butter, melted

12 to 13 servings

Place the spinach in a microwave-safe container and thaw completely. Spinach can also be cooked, until thawed, in a saucepan. Squeeze all excess moisture out in paper towels or by putting the spinach in a potato ricer and pressing. Transfer it to a large bowl.

Add the oil, scallions, parsley, dill, eggs, and cheese. Mix until well blended. Season with salt and pepper.

Spread the stack of phyllo on a work surface and cover with three sheets of paper towel that have been wet, then wrung out until nearly dry.

Brush a baking dish, about 10 x 13 inches, with a little of the butter. Place a sheet of the phyllo into the dish, spread lightly with butter, add another sheet of phyllo, brush with butter, and continue until there are 8 sheets in the dish. Spread the spinach mixture into the dish, then top with another 8 sheets of phyllo, buttering each as it is added. Butter the top.

With a sharp knife, score the top sheets of phyllo, down to the filling, making about 20 squares, 2½ inches across. Then cut each on the diagonal, to make about 40 triangles.

Preheat the oven to 350 degrees.

Sprinkle the top of the phyllo with a little water and place in the oven. Bake 45 to 55 minutes, until golden. Allow to cool 15 minutes, then cut through where the phyllo was scored. Arrange the triangles on a platter and serve.

Using phyllo is simple, once you try it. It is important to allow it to thaw completely, preferably in the refrigerator, before using it, so it will be perfectly pliable. Do not worry if some sheets break or tear a bit, since you are not wrapping individual triangles of the phyllo but just piling the sheets in the baking dish, and breakage will not show. You can, or course, make individual triangles. For each you will need one-third of a sheet cut the long way. You brush the strip with butter, fold it in half the long way, and place a teaspoon or two of the filling at the bottom of the strip. Then fold it into a triangle, over and over, just the way you would fold an American flag. You can bake the triangles on a cookie sheet until they have browned.

SOUPS FOR
ALL SEASONS

FAVORITE TOMATO SOUP

ALI'S CHILLED MINTED PEA SOUP

CURRIED PEA SOUP

SUMMERTIME ZUCCHINI SOUP

BLUSHING CRAB SOUP

HEARTY LENTIL SOUP

Left: Ali's Chilled Minted Pea Soup

Favorite Tomato Soup

*T*HIS RECIPE ORIGINALLY CAME FROM MY GODMOTHER AND WAS MADE BY MY MOTHER OVER THE YEARS WHEN I WAS GROWING UP. I NOW MAKE IT QUITE OFTEN MYSELF, AND IT BRINGS BACK FOND MEMORIES OF COLD WINTER DAYS IN CONNECTICUT. MY MOTHER WOULD SERVE IT WITH WARM FRENCH BREAD, WHICH WAS PERFECT FOR DIPPING INTO THE SOUP. I STILL DO THE SAME OR HAVE IT WITH A SALAD, BUT MY ABSOLUTE FAVORITE IS TO PAIR IT WITH A GRILLED CHEESE SANDWICH—SOURDOUGH WITH CHEDDAR IS THE VERY BEST WITH THIS SOUP, ESPECIALLY ON A CHILLY SUNDAY.

THE INGREDIENTS FOR THIS EASY SOUP ARE SOLD AT ANY GROCERY STORE. IT IS VERSATILE ENOUGH TO SATISFY A CASUAL FAMILY LUNCH, AN AUTUMN TAILGATE PICNIC, OR AN ELEGANT DINNER PARTY. THOUGH IT IS GOOD ANY TIME OF YEAR, I LIKE IT BEST HOT, SO I TEND TO MAKE IT IN COOLER WEATHER. IT CAN BE SERVED CHILLED, HOWEVER, FOR A REFRESHING SUMMER TREAT WHEN BASIL IS AT ITS BEST.

2 TABLESPOONS EXTRA VIRGIN OLIVE OIL

2 TABLESPOONS UNSALTED BUTTER

1 CUP CHOPPED ONION

2 POUNDS FRESH, RIPE PLUM TOMATOES, PEELED, SEEDED, AND QUARTERED (SEE OPPOSITE), OR 2 CANS (28 OUNCES EACH) CRUSHED PLUM TOMATOES

1½ CUPS CHICKEN OR VEGETABLE STOCK

2 TABLESPOONS TOMATO PASTE

1 TEASPOON SUGAR

SALT AND FRESHLY GROUND BLACK PEPPER

1 TEASPOON FRESH THYME LEAVES, OR ½ TEASPOON DRIED

1 TABLESPOON FINELY MINCED FRESH BASIL, IF AVAILABLE, PLUS SPRIGS FOR GARNISH, OPTIONAL

1 CUP CROUTONS

½ CUP SOUR CREAM OR CRÈME FRAÎCHE, OPTIONAL

8 SERVINGS

Heat the oil and butter in a heavy 4-quart pot. Add the onion and sauté it over low heat until it softens. If you are using fresh tomatoes, pulse them in your food processor until they are finely chopped. Add them to the pot, or add canned tomatoes if those are what you are using. Add the chicken stock and tomato paste and bring everything to a simmer. Season the soup with sugar, salt, and pepper. Add thyme and, if you are using it, the fresh basil. Continue to simmer for 30 minutes.

Serve the soup at once, topped with croutons and a dollop of sour cream or crème fraîche, if desired, and basil sprigs, if they're available. The soup can also be set aside (without toppings) and reheated later.

NOTE: For an unusual and sophisticated hors d'oeuvre, you can puree the soup in a blender until it's smooth. Then return it to the pot, add 1 cup of heavy cream, bring it to a simmer, and cook another 5 minutes. Serve the soup spooned into little espresso cups and passed on a tray, without saucers or spoons. You could also serve the soup this way, with the cream, chilled instead of hot. Or, for a show-stopping first course, you could present warmed soup plates with just a slice of cooked lobster in each, then ladle the soup in at the table—a restaurant touch that is always effective.

Peeling fresh plum tomatoes is easy. Simply bring a big pot of water to a boil. Cut a shallow X into the bottom of each tomato, just to break the skin, and drop into the boiling water, in batches, for just one minute. Remove the tomatoes to a big bowl of cold water to stop the cooking. The skin around the X should be loosened enough that, once cool enough to handle, the tomatoes are easily skinned.

All it takes to make croutons from scratch is to remove the crusts from 4 slices of firm whole wheat or white bread and cut the slices into ½-inch cubes. In a skillet, heat 2 tablespoons of olive oil over medium heat and sauté the cubes, stirring frequently until lightly browned. They're perfectly delicious as is, but also feel free to season or toss them with any blend of herbs you like.

Ali's Chilled Minted Pea Soup

*T*HIS SOUP IS NAMED FOR THE FRIEND WHO GAVE THE RECIPE TO ME. I MAKE A BATCH OF IT EVERY WEEK IN THE SUMMER AND SOMETIMES DOUBLE IT, DEPENDING ON HOW MANY HOUSE GUESTS OR LUNCH OR DINNER GUESTS WE MAY HAVE. IT IS THE PERFECT APPETIZER FOR AN AL FRESCO DINNER OR SERVED WITH SOME WARM, HOMEMADE BREAD AS A VERY CASUAL LUNCH ENTRÉE FOR "THE GIRLS." BEFORE SERVING, PUT THE CUPS OR BOWLS YOU PLAN TO USE IN THE REFRIGERATOR FOR AN HOUR, TO HELP THE SOUP KEEP ITS CHILL WHILE YOUR GUESTS ARE SPOONING IT UP. AND CONSIDER GIVING THIS SOUP THE HORS D'OEUVRE TREATMENT, IN ESPRESSO CUPS, AS SUGGESTED IN THE NOTE FOR FAVORITE TOMATO SOUP ON PAGE 67.

THIS IS A VERSATILE RECIPE THAT CAN EASILY BE VARIED. FOR EXAMPLE, TO GIVE IT A LUSTY MEXICAN ACCENT, REPLACE THE MINT WITH FRESH CILANTRO LEAVES, ADD HALF A FRESH, SEEDED JALAPEÑO CHILI (OR TO TASTE), USE SOUR CREAM, AND SERVE TORTILLA CHIPS ALONGSIDE.

1 POUND FROZEN BABY GREEN PEAS

2 CUPS CHICKEN STOCK

2 SMALL SCALLIONS, TRIMMED AND COARSELY CHOPPED

2 TABLESPOONS FRESH LIME JUICE

1/2 TEASPOON GROUND NUTMEG, PREFERABLY FRESHLY GRATED

14 FRESH MINT LEAVES, PLUS MORE FOR GARNISH

1/2 CUP THICK WHOLE MILK YOGURT OR SOUR CREAM,
PLUS MORE FOR GARNISH

SALT AND FRESHLY GROUND BLACK PEPPER

4 SERVINGS

Place the peas in a blender. Heat the chicken stock to boiling, pour it over the peas, and puree. Add the scallions, lime juice, nutmeg, and mint and blend. Add the yogurt or sour cream and blend again until smooth.

Season to taste with salt and pepper. Chill at least 3 hours. Check seasoning again and serve in bowls or cups, each garnished with a small dollop of yogurt or sour cream and a mint leaf.

NOTE: The best yogurt for this recipe is thick, Greek-style. It adds an appetite-whetting tang to the soup, making for a particularly refreshing starter in hot weather. To use it as a garnish, stir it first so it will be smooth. Sour cream, the other option, is richer. You choose.

The near impossibility of finding fresh baby peas, even in early summer, makes using frozen peas an essential expedient and worthwhile alternative. The magic in this recipe is the way the hot broth actually "cooks" the frozen peas in the blender, so no thawing is necessary. Just be sure to buy frozen peas that are not in any sauce; and you will have an easier time if they are loose in the package, not in a solid block. Give the package a good whack on the countertop to loosen the peas, if necessary.

Curried Pea Soup

*I*JUST LOVE THE BRIGHT GREEN COLOR OF THIS SOUP—IT ALWAYS REMINDS ME OF SPRING. AND THE SIMPLE FLAVORS, BOLSTERED WITH A WHIFF OF CURRY, REALLY POP. WHAT A GREAT WAY TO START A MEAL! AT THE SAME TIME, THE CURRY CAN BE OMITTED AND THE SOUP WILL ALSO BE DELICIOUS. IT CAN BE SERVED HOT OR COLD, BUT BE SURE TO REMEMBER TO BE GENEROUS WITH YOUR SEASONINGS IF YOU SERVE IT COLD BECAUSE THE CHILL WILL DULL THEM. THE SOUP IS EASY TO MAKE AND CONVENIENT BECAUSE THE INGREDIENTS ARE READILY AVAILABLE. I ALWAYS LOOK FOR ORGANIC INGREDIENTS IN MY SUPERMARKET. I ALSO LIKE TO VARY THE GARNISHES TO ADD A LEVEL OF SOPHISTICATION. SOUR CREAM, YOGURT, LITTLE GRILLED SHRIMP, SOME CRABMEAT, GARLIC CROUTONS, SLIVERS OF CURED HAM LIKE JAMÓN SERRANO, CRUMBLED BACON, OR A DOLLOP OF CHUTNEY ARE JUST A FEW IDEAS. YOU MIGHT CONSIDER PASSING A TRAY OF LITTLE DISHES, EACH WITH A DIFFERENT GARNISH, MUCH THE WAY GAZPACHO IS OFTEN SERVED, SO GUESTS CAN CUSTOM-DECORATE TO TASTE. OR YOU MIGHT EVEN CONSIDER DROPLETS OF SEASONED OIL FLOATING ON THE SURFACE OF EACH PORTION OF SOUP.

8 SERVINGS

2 TABLESPOONS EXTRA VIRGIN OLIVE OIL

1 MEDIUM ONION, FINELY SLICED

1 HEAD ROMAINE LETTUCE, CORED AND FINELY SLICED (ABOUT 6 CUPS)

2 TABLESPOONS CURRY POWDER

1 1/2 QUARTS CHICKEN STOCK

3 CUPS PEAS, FRESH OR FROZEN

1/2 CUP FLAT-LEAF PARSLEY LEAVES

SEA SALT AND FRESHLY GROUND BLACK PEPPER

4 TEASPOONS LEMON JUICE

In a large pot, heat the oil over low heat and sauté the onion until pale and soft. Add the lettuce and continue to sauté until wilted. Add the curry and stir to combine well and release the aroma of curry. Pour in the chicken broth, peas, and parsley. Season with salt and pepper to taste.

Bring to a boil, lower the heat, and simmer until the peas are tender. In a blender or food processor, puree the soup in batches until smooth. Return the soup to a clean saucepan and reheat it gently. Check the seasonings, add lemon juice, and serve with a garnish.

To serve the soup cold, chill it for at least 3 hours; check the seasonings and add the lemon juice just before serving. Add a garnish of your choice to each serving.

It is important to heat the curry powder in the oil with some of the ingredients before adding the liquid: many spices like curry need to react with heat and fat of some kind to mellow them and eliminate their raw taste. The scintilla of acidity that the lemon juice contributes also punches up the flavor of the soup. But whether the soup is to be served hot or cold, the lemon should be added just before serving because otherwise it will dull the beautiful verdant color of the soup. Also, the color will be less vibrant if the soup is made more than a few hours in advance. Another pointer worth remembering is that if the soup is to be served cold, it is important to use oil instead of butter to sauté your ingredients because butter, when chilled, will coagulate and could be unpleasant to eat. And olive oil is fine for a hot soup, too.

Summertime Zucchini Soup

We were motoring out West one summer, and we stopped at a friend's house in Aspen, Colorado. On her terrace overlooking the mountains, she served an excellent lunch that started with this delicious soup. Of course, I asked for the recipe, and I have made it part of my repertoire. I serve it either hot, often topped with croutons, or cold with a sprinkling of chives.

Like other pureed soups designed to be served hot or cold, this one will take to a variety of garnishes—but not all at once! Other possibilities from those suggested here include a scattering of slivered or sliced toasted almonds, tiny bright dicings of sweet yellow or red bell pepper, and even a dab of olive tapenade or, for a real touch of luxury, a small mound of farmed sturgeon caviar from California parked in the center of the zucchini slice.

3 pounds medium-small zucchini (not baby zucchini), trimmed

6 tablespoons extra virgin olive oil or unsalted butter

1/3 cup chopped shallots

1 tablespoon curry powder

Salt and freshly ground black pepper

4 1/2 cups chicken stock

1 1/2 cups low-fat or whole milk

3 tablespoons crème fraîche, optional

2 tablespoons minced chives or 1/2 cup small croutons

6 TO 8 SERVINGS

Slice the zucchini, reserving 6 to 8 of the slices, depending on the number of servings, for garnish.

Melt the oil or butter in a large saucepan. Add the shallots and cook over low heat until soft but not brown. Stir in the curry powder and zucchini. Season with salt and pepper, cover, and cook 10 to 15 minutes, until zucchini are soft. Stir in the chicken stock and milk.

Puree the mixture in a blender, in batches. Return the soup to a clean saucepan and whisk in the crème fraîche if using. Check seasonings. Reheat the soup if serving hot, or chill it at least 3 hours to serve cold.

Float one of the reserved zucchini slices on each serving and top with chives or croutons.

NOTE: This soup can be gossamer-light if you prepare it using the oil instead of butter and, in place of the milk, more chicken stock. But then you really need the small amount of crème fraîche to add just a spark of richness. The touch of curry powder is barely noticeable, adding neither color nor sharp flavor, but contributing an intriguing element of complexity to the end result.

Summer and early fall, when the farm stands and gardens overflow with freshly picked zucchini, is when this soup begs to be made. Though selecting uniform-size, smallish zucchini may not seem important when the vegetable will be pureed anyway, it is critical to the success of this soup. Smaller zucchini will have denser flesh, fewer seeds, and be much less watery. And because there is a higher ratio of skin to flesh when the zucchini are small, the color of the soup will be more vibrant. Of course, buy unbruised zucchini that feel very firm.

Blushing Crab Soup

*T*HE RECIPE FOR THIS SOUP, WHICH IS MY FAVORITE FIRST COURSE TO SERVE AT DINNER PARTIES, WAS GIVEN TO ME BY ANNIE BREED, WHO WAS A MEMBER OF THE SOCIETY FOR MANY YEARS. WHAT I LOVE ABOUT THIS SOUP IS THAT IT CAN BE MADE AHEAD OF TIME, EVEN THE DAY BEFORE, AND KEPT REFRIGERATED UNTIL NEAR SERVING TIME. BUT IF YOU DO THAT, WAIT WITH THE CREAM AND THE CRABMEAT AND ADD THEM DURING THE FINAL REHEATING. ALSO BE SURE TO TASTE THE SOUP AND CORRECT THE SEASONING BEFORE YOU SERVE IT.

THIS SOUP COULD CERTAINLY BE PUREED, BEFORE ADDING THE CREAM AND THE CRABMEAT, TO SMOOTH IT TO A VELVETY BISQUE. THEN IT'S SUITABLE FOR THE MOST FORMAL OF DINNER PARTIES. STILL, THE BIT OF TEXTURE THE SOUP HAS WITHOUT THE BLENDER TREATMENT GIVES IT AN HONEST, HOMEY QUALITY THAT NICELY BALANCES THE LUXURY OF ITS INGREDIENTS. FOR THAT MATTER, BEFORE THE CRABMEAT IS ADDED YOU HAVE A SOUP THAT IS A BIT OF A BLANK SLATE. SO IF YOU ARE INSPIRED TO ADD SLICED BAY SCALLOPS, DICED LOBSTER MEAT, OR EVEN SLIVERS OF SMOKED SALMON INSTEAD OF CRABMEAT, GO RIGHT AHEAD. BUT IF YOU DO USE THE SALMON, ADD IT AT THE VERY LAST MINUTE, AFTER THE REHEATING AND JUST BEFORE YOU SERVE THE SOUP.

The distinction that was made fifty to seventy-five years ago between cream soups, bouillons, and other soups, down to the shape of the bowl and spoon—deeper and more cuplike bowls with two handles for cream soups and bouillons, with spoons that were rounded—have all but disappeared. This soup will be perfectly beautiful ladled into a flat soup plate. If you portion it out in the kitchen, be sure to take a piece of damp paper towel to wipe any accidental drips on the rim of the plate. If you serve it at the table from a handsome tureen, be extra careful.

6 SERVINGS

4 TABLESPOONS UNSALTED BUTTER

1/2 CUP FINELY CHOPPED ONION

I CLOVE GARLIC, FINELY MINCED

1/2 GRANNY SMITH APPLE, PEELED, CORED AND FINELY CHOPPED

I 1/2 TEASPOONS CURRY POWDER

1/4 CUP FLOUR

1/2 CUP PEELED, SEEDED, AND DICED TOMATO (SEE SIDEBAR, PAGE 43)

3 CUPS CHICKEN STOCK

SALT AND FRESHLY GROUND BLACK PEPPER

1/2 CUP HEAVY CREAM

1/2 POUND LUMP CRABMEAT, CAREFULLY PICKED OVER

TABASCO SAUCE OR CAYENNE TO TASTE

I TABLESPOON MINCED FLAT-LEAF PARSLEY LEAVES

Melt the butter in a saucepan. Add the onion and cook, stirring, until soft. Add the garlic and apple. Stir briefly and sprinkle with the curry powder and flour. Cook for about a minute. Stir in the tomato.

Add the chicken stock, stirring rapidly with a wire whisk until smooth and thickened. Simmer briefly and then add salt and pepper to taste. Whisk in the cream. Gently stir in the crabmeat and simmer for 10 minutes.

Add a touch of Tabasco or cayenne to sharpen the flavor. Serve hot with a little parsley to garnish each serving.

Hearty Lentil Soup

M MOTHER WAS FROM CUBA, WHERE LEGUMES ARE NOT ONLY A STAPLE, BUT ALMOST THE BEST PART OF ANY MEAL. MY MOM LIKED TO COOK LENTILS INSTEAD OF THE USUAL BLACK OR RED BEANS. FOR ONE THING, THEY DO NOT HAVE TO BE SOAKED AS LONG. AND SHE WOULD ALSO ADD SHREDDED BEEF, HAM, OR SAUSAGE FOR A COMPLETE, HEALTHY, AND HEARTY WINTER DINNER. SHE WOULD SERVE IT IN LARGE SOUP BOWLS, WITH FRIED GREEN BANANAS AND CRUSTY BREAD ALONGSIDE. AND OF COURSE, GLASSES OF RED WINE. IT WAS HEAVEN. I LIKE A BIBB LETTUCE SALAD AND GOAT CHEESE WITH IT. SOMETIMES, I CUT BACK ON THE AMOUNT OF LIQUID, REDUCING THE STOCK TO ONLY TWO TO THREE CUPS, AND SERVE IT OVER RICE, LIKE CHILI. IT'S STILL ONE OF MY FAVORITE DINNERS.

1 POUND LENTILS, PREFERABLY FRENCH GREEN LE PUY, RINSED

1 TABLESPOON UNSALTED BUTTER

1/2 POUND PROSCIUTTO, DICED SMALL

1 CARROT, TRIMMED, PEELED, AND SLICED

1/2 CUP FINELY CHOPPED ONION

1/2 CUP FINELY CHOPPED CELERY

1 CLOVE GARLIC, MINCED

5 TO 6 CUPS CHICKEN OR VEGETABLE STOCK, OR MORE, AS NEEDED

SALT AND FRESHLY GROUND BLACK PEPPER

1/3 CUP FLAT-LEAF PARSLEY LEAVES, FINELY CHOPPED

Place the lentils in a large bowl, cover with cold water, and let them soak for about 4 hours. Drain and set them aside.

In a large pot, melt the butter. Add the ham and let it cook over low heat for a few minutes. Add the carrots, onion, and celery and let them cook until tender but not browned, about 6 minutes. Stir in the garlic, the lentils, and 5 cups of the chicken stock.

Bring to a simmer, lower the heat, partly cover the pot, and let everything simmer for about 45 minutes, until the lentils are tender.

Add additional chicken stock to adjust the texture of the soup. It should be thick, but definitely soupy. If you prepare the soup in advance and then reheat it, you may have to add additional stock.

Check the seasonings and serve, garnished with parsley.

If you are looking for a dish to serve for a New Year's Day buffet, this soup heads the list. In many cultures, including Italian, lentils and dried beans are considered good luck, guarantees of wealth and prosperity for the New Year. You can keep it in a tureen or even a deep pot, like an enameled cast-iron casserole, on a warmer on the buffet table. Just be sure to check from time to time that it has not thickened too much as it stands, and keep some extra warm chicken stock in the kitchen to stir in if needed. A varied cheese board could also go alongside. A stack of mugs instead of soup bowls or soup plates will take up less room on your buffet table; mugs will also be easier for your guests to manage, and they add a nicely rustic touch to the service.

The finest lentils are the smallish, rounded green LePuy lentils from central France. Their texture is particularly welcome in this soup since it is not pureed. However, there are other types of lentils worth considering. Do you want the soup to match your dining room décor, or your dinnerware? Consider pinkish Champagne lentils, also from France, and another variety worth trying. Indian lentils come in orange or yellow, and the newest are chic black beluga lentils.

SALADS OF SUBSTANCE

AVOCADOES ARGENTINA

THE NEW COBB SALAD

CHICKEN SALAD FOR THE LADIES

TURKEY TONNATO

PASTA SALAD WITH PESTO

SOCIETY SALMON MOLD

Left: Chicken Salad for the Ladies

Avocadoes Argentina

My mother-in-law, Isabel Fowlkes, gave me this recipe as part of a collection that was a gift one Christmas. I was recently married and a total novice in the kitchen. This recipe is one of our favorites. It is a dish that Isabel particularly loved when she was growing up in Argentina.

Shrimp can be substituted for crabmeat and instead of plain mayonnaise, you can add a little ketchup to make a Russian dressing. You can make the seafood salad simpler by omitting the celery and tomato, or vary it in other ways, too. For a buffet, consider doubling or tripling the recipe and arranging the stuffed avocado halves on a platter.

8 ounces lump crabmeat

1 medium ripe tomato, diced

1 stalk celery, diced

1 teaspoon fresh tarragon leaves, minced

1/4 cup mayonnaise

Juice of 1 lemon

Salt and freshly ground black pepper

3 avocados

1 tablespoon minced chives

2 bunches arugula, stems removed, or 2 heads Bibb lettuce,
coarsely shredded

3 tablespoons extra virgin olive oil

Pick over the crabmeat to remove any bits of cartilage. Combine the crabmeat, tomato, celery, fresh tarragon, mayonnaise, and 1 teaspoon of the lemon juice in a bowl. Season to taste with salt and pepper.

Halve and pit the avocadoes. Brush the cut sides with a tablespoon of the lemon juice.

Pile the crabmeat mixture in the cavity of each avocado half; garnish each with about ½ teaspoon of the chives.

Place the arugula or lettuce in a mixing bowl.

Beat the olive oil with the remaining lemon juice. Pour over the arugula or lettuce, add the remaining chives and toss. Season with salt and pepper. Divide this salad on 6 salad plates, place a crab-stuffed avocado on each, and serve.

It's easy to see how this dish can become a repertory classic. Not only can shrimp be used instead of crabmeat, but a chicken salad, a fish salad, even, for a lighter dish, a marinated seafood ceviche can be piled into the avocado. The simplest ceviche is made with very fresh diced raw flounder or other mild, fresh fish, including red snapper. Use 8 ounces of the fish, as in the recipe, with the other ingredients, but substitute ¼ cup lime juice for the mayonnaise. And unlike many ceviche recipes, the fish does not have to marinate overnight until the acid in the lime juice "cooks" it. A mere 30 minutes will do, as tastes now accept raw fish, like sushi and sashimi.

The New Cobb Salad

THIS RECIPE WAS DEVELOPED BY THE AMERICANA RESTAURANT AT THE RITZ-CARLTON SOUTH BEACH IN MIAMI. THE INGREDIENTS ARE ALL THE THINGS YOU'D FIND IN A STANDARD COBB SALAD—THEY'RE MY FAVORITES—BUT GIVEN A STYLISH TWIST. I NEVER MISS AN OPPORTUNITY TO ORDER THIS SALAD WHEN I AM AT THE POOL AT THE HOTEL AND HAVING LUNCH WITH MY CHILDREN. IT'S LIGHT AND FRESH AND DELICIOUS, LOW IN CALORIES, AND THE FLAVORS JUST BLOSSOM ON THE PALATE.

THE SALAD WAS ORIGINALLY DESIGNED AS A SINGLE SERVING, WITH THE INGREDIENTS LAYERED IN A ROUND TUBE MOLD, THE SORT OF THING CHEFS USE, LIKE A TUNAFISH CAN OPEN AT BOTH ENDS. YOU REMOVE THE CAN AND YOU HAVE THE INGREDIENTS IN A LOVELY CYLINDER. PREPARING IT THIS WAY IS TIME-CONSUMING, BUT NOT OUT OF THE QUESTION, AS A LUNCHEON DISH OR A FIRST COURSE FOR FOUR, FIVE, OR SIX PEOPLE. BUT WITH THE INGREDIENTS BEAUTIFULLY ARRANGED IN CONCENTRIC CIRCLES ON A PLATTER, IT IS EXCELLENT ON A BUFFET, ESPECIALLY IF YOU HAVE SOMEONE SERVE IT. IF YOU DISH IT OUT YOURSELF, TRY TO KEEP THE INGREDIENTS NEATLY ARRANGED AS PORTIONS ARE REMOVED.

3/4 CUP EXTRA VIRGIN OLIVE OIL

3/4 CUP LIME JUICE, ABOUT 6 LIMES

1 TABLESPOON SUGAR

SALT AND FRESHLY GROUND BLACK PEPPER, TO TASTE

3 AVOCADOES, PITTED, PEELED, AND DICED

4 LARGE RIPE HEIRLOOM TOMATOES, PEELED, CORED, AND SLICED 1/8 INCH THICK
(SEE SIDEBAR, PAGE 67)

2 LOGS (8 OUNCES EACH) GOAT CHEESE, SLICED

1 1/2 POUNDS COOKED LOBSTER MEAT, DICED

12 QUAIL EGGS, HARD BOILED, PEELED, AND HALVED

1 1/2 POUNDS MÂCHE LETTUCE, ROOTS TRIMMED, RINSED, AND DRIED

1 POUND PROSCIUTTO, SLICED

Beat the olive oil, lime juice, and sugar together. Season with salt and pepper. Toss the avocadoes with one-third of the dressing.

Arrange the tomato slices, overlapping, around the outside of a very large platter. Season with salt and pepper. Spoon the avocado around the platter in the center of the tomato slices. Place a circle of the goat cheese, the slices slightly overlapping, just inside the avocado. Season the goat cheese with pepper.

Toss the lobster with one-third of the dressing and place it just inside the goat cheese. Garnish evenly with the quail egg halves. The very center of the platter should still be empty.

Toss the mâche with the remaining dressing and pile it into the center of the platter. Roll the prosciutto slices into cylinders and lean them against the pile of greens, like spokes of a wheel. Serve.

Many seafood markets sell cooked lobster meat. But at a price. You can save money by preparing your own. For a pound and a half of meat, you will need four 1-pound lobsters. They are the cheapest to buy and because the shells are not too thick, they are the easiest to handle, assuming you do not mind dropping live lobsters into boiling water. Bring a stockpot filled with water to a boil, drop in the lobsters, cover, and allow them to cook for 3 minutes. Boiling is the quickest way to cook a lobster, much faster than steaming or broiling. The lobsters will have turned red. Remove them and allow them to cool until you can handle them. Crack the shells and remove the tail meat and the claw meat and even the meat in the knuckles that are attached to the claws. Dice it for the recipe.

Chicken Salad for the Ladies

THIS IS YOUR BASIC CHICKEN SALAD THAT I LIKE TO DOLL UP WITH OTHER INGREDIENTS. I'VE ADDED NUTS, CHUTNEY, AND APRICOTS OVER THE YEARS. IT'S A FRESH ALTERNATIVE TO CURRIED CHICKEN SALAD. I SERVE IT WHEN IT'S MY TURN TO HOST A CELEBRATORY LUNCH FOR MY TENNIS GROUP AT THE END OF THE SEASON. I SERVE THE SALAD FROM A LARGE, SHALLOW CHINA BOWL, OFTEN WITH A BRIGHT GREEN VEGETABLE SALAD, LIKE A COLD BROCCOLI SALAD WITH BACON, ALONGSIDE. I SET THE LUNCHEON TABLE WITH MY WEDDING CHINA, WHICH IS PINK AND APPLE GREEN. AND SOME OF MY SILVER SERVING PIECES ARE FAMILY HEIRLOOMS IN A DOGWOOD PATTERN, SO IN THE SPRING, I USE DOGWOOD BRANCHES FOR DECORATION. WE'RE FROM VIRGINIA, AND IT'S OUR STATE FLOWER.

A SHORTCUT TO THIS RECIPE IS TO PURCHASE A ROTISSERIE CHICKEN OR COOKED CHICKEN BREASTS FROM A PREPARED FOOD SHOP AND USE THEM INSTEAD OF COOKING THE CHICKEN FROM SCRATCH. YOU CAN ADJUST THE PROPORTIONS OF THE DRESSING TO TASTE, USING MORE OR LESS MAYONNAISE OR YOGURT. SIMILARLY, YOU CAN SUIT YOURSELF AS TO THE AMOUNT OF CHUTNEY.

When you are mixing a salad or, for that matter, any other combination of ingredients, always try to use a large bowl, one that allows plenty of room to toss the ingredients. Then once everything is well combined, you can transfer the salad to the serving bowl or arrange it on individual plates, with some of the garnish topping each serving.

10 TO 12 SERVINGS

4 POUNDS BONELESS AND SKINLESS CHICKEN BREASTS

SALT AND FRESHLY GROUND BLACK PEPPER

1 1/2 CUPS CHOPPED SCALLIONS

1 1/2 CUPS FINELY CHOPPED CELERY

2 MANGOES, PEELED, SEEDED, AND DICED

1/2 CUP MAJOR GREY'S MANGO CHUTNEY (SEE SIDEBAR, PAGE 47)

1 CUP MAYONNAISE

JUICE OF 2 LEMONS

3 CUPS WHOLE MILK YOGURT

2 TABLESPOONS SOY SAUCE

1/2 CUP SALTED PEANUTS, FINELY CHOPPED

1/3 CUP CHOPPED CILANTRO LEAVES

Preheat the oven to 300 degrees. Line a large roasting pan or jelly-roll pan with foil, place the chicken breasts in the pan in a single layer, season with salt and pepper, and cover with foil. Place in the oven and bake until the chicken is just cooked through, about 30 minutes. Remove chicken and allow to cool.

Meanwhile, in a very large bowl, combine the scallions, celery, mangoes, chutney, mayonnaise, lemon juice, yogurt, and soy sauce. Mix well. Combine the peanuts and cilantro together in a small bowl and reserve this mixture.

When the chicken is cool enough to handle, chop it with a knife in bite-size pieces. Add it to the bowl and fold it in with the other ingredients.

To serve, transfer the salad to a shallow bowl or a platter and garnish the top with the peanut mixture.

NOTE: There is a new gadget on the market designed for slicing and pitting a mango, and if you like to serve mangoes, it pays to have one on hand.

Turkey Tonnato

I CANNOT REMEMBER WHERE I GOT THIS RECIPE. I'VE BEEN SERVING IT FOR ABOUT TWENTY YEARS AND MY GUESTS LOVE IT. BECAUSE I DO NOT EAT RED MEAT—EVEN VEAL, WHICH IS THE BASIS FOR THE ORIGINAL RECIPE, VITELLO TONNATO—THIS VERSION APPEALS TO ME. THE MAIN FLAVORING COMES FROM THE SAUCE, NOT THE MEAT. VITELLO TONNATO MADE WITH TURKEY HAS BEEN ON THE MENU AT THE CIPRIANI RESTAURANTS, STARTING WITH HARRY'S BAR IN VENICE.

1 CAN (6$\frac{1}{2}$ OUNCES) IMPORTED TUNA IN OIL, DRAINED

3 TABLESPOONS DRAINED CAPERS

1$\frac{1}{2}$ CUPS MAYONNAISE

1 TEASPOON LEMON JUICE

1 TABLESPOON FINELY CHOPPED ANCHOVY FILLETS, OR ANCHOVY PASTE

2 TABLESPOONS CHICKEN BROTH OR DRY WHITE WINE

1 POUND COOKED, BONELESS TURKEY, SLICED ABOUT $\frac{1}{8}$ INCH THICK

FOR GARNISH:

SEEDED THIN LEMON SLICES

BLACK OLIVES IN OIL

FINELY CHOPPED PARSLEY

6 TO 8 SERVINGS

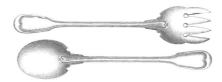

Put the tuna and capers into the container of a food processor or electric blender and blend. Add the mayonnaise, lemon juice, anchovies, and stock or wine. Blend thoroughly.

Spread a thin layer of the mayonnaise mixture on a serving platter. Place about a third of the turkey slices, slightly overlapping, on the sauce. Spoon another layer of sauce on top. Add another layer of turkey slices and more sauce. Make one more layer, finishing with a layer of sauce. Arrange lemon slices and olives on the top and scatter with parsley. Refrigerate it, covered, until 1 hour before serving time. Allow the dish to come to room temperature before serving.

This recipe can be made totally from scratch by roasting a whole or half turkey breast, then cutting slices once it has cooled. Certainly, if you plan the dish for one or two platters at a large buffet—for twenty or more servings—it's what you should do. Otherwise, buy good-quality cooked turkey breast, the kind that food shops roast themselves, not from a roll or a package. The slices should not be paper thin. As for the tuna, the only kind worth using for this recipe is imported, packed preferably in olive oil. There are many brands on the market from Italy, Spain, and Portugal.

BARBARA TOLLIS

Pasta Salad with Pesto

*I*FIRST TASTED PESTO IN THE 1970S IN A SMALL RESTAURANT IN NEW YORK'S LITTLE ITALY, AND I'VE BEEN HOOKED EVER SINCE. A SALAD OF PASTA WITH PESTO BECAME PART OF ONE OF MY FAVORITE SUMMER RECIPES TO SERVE AT OUR BIG WICKER TABLE IN SOUTHAMPTON, AND ANY LEFTOVERS WOULD BE TAKEN TO THE BEACH THE NEXT DAY OR BACK TO THE CITY AFTER THE WEEKEND. I HAD MY SOURCES FOR FRESH BASIL, PINE NUTS, MOZZARELLA, AND PROSCIUTTO. THE FRESH CORN ON THE COB AND TOMATOES THAT I WOULD SERVE WITH THE SALAD ALWAYS CAME FROM A LOCAL FARM.

ANOTHER WAY TO PRESENT THIS SALAD IS TO OMIT THE MOZZARELLA AND PROSCIUTTO FROM THE MIXTURE AND SERVE THEM IN SLICES, ALONGSIDE. IF YOU DISH THE SALAD ONTO INDIVIDUAL PLATES, THERE CAN BE A SLICE OF THE PROSCIUTTO AND ONE OF THE MOZZARELLA ON EACH PLATE. RESERVE A LITTLE OF YOUR PESTO AND DRIZZLE JUST A BIT OF IT ON THE CHEESE. RIPE, FRESH TOMATOES AND CRUSTY COUNTRY BREAD ARE WHAT YOU NEED ALONGSIDE.

FOR THE PESTO:

2 CLOVES GARLIC

1 1/2 CUPS PACKED, FRESH BASIL LEAVES (ABOUT 1 BUNCH),
PLUS A FEW SPRIGS FOR GARNISH

1/3 CUP PINE NUTS

3/4 CUP EXTRA VIRGIN OLIVE OIL

1/2 CUP GRATED PARMIGIANO-REGGIANO

SALT AND FRESHLY GROUND BLACK PEPPER

1 POUND FUSILLI PASTA

2 CUPS FRESH PEAS OR 1 BOX (10 OUNCES) FROZEN PEAS

1 POUND FRESH, LIGHTLY SALTED MOZZARELLA, DICED

1/2 POUND PROSCIUTTO IN 4 THICK SLICES, DICED

10 SERVINGS

To make the fresh pesto, first turn on a food processor. Drop the garlic cloves into the machine through the feed tube and process until the garlic is minced. Scrape down the sides of the bowl, and then place basil leaves in the bowl and pulse until finely chopped. Add the nuts and pulse until chopped. With the machine running, slowly pour the olive oil in through the feed tube to make a fine, rich green puree. Transfer this mixture to a bowl, fold in the Parmigiano-Reggiano, and season to taste with salt and pepper.

Bring a large pot of salted water to a boil for the pasta. Add the fusilli and fresh peas, if you are using them, and cook both about 8 minutes, until tender. Drain well in a colander. With frozen peas, add them just before the pasta is finished cooking.

Transfer the pasta and the peas to a large bowl. Fold in the mozzarella and prosciutto. Fold in the pesto.

Serve at room temperature, or refrigerate, and allow to come to room temperature for 1 hour before serving. Garnish with basil sprigs.

The pesto part of the recipe will yield about 1½ cups of the sauce. You can always purchase prepared pesto, but if fresh basil is available, making it from scratch could not be simpler. Just be sure to use genuine Italian imported Parmigiano-Reggiano, not some kind of generic "parmesan." As for the prosciutto, there, too, it pays to look for the imported kind, though there are some excellent artisanal producers in the United States now, including one in Iowa, one in California, and one, who happens to be chef Mario Batali's father, in Seattle.

Society Salmon Mold

I HOLD MANY, MANY LUNCHEONS FOR MEMBERS OF THE SOCIETY, AND I ALWAYS SERVE A MOLD OR A TERRINE OF SOME KIND. IT HAS BECOME MY SIGNATURE. THIS ONE, USING SALMON, IS ONE OF THE MOST POPULAR. THE RECIPE WAS ORIGINALLY GIVEN TO ME BY THE WOMAN WHO WAS MY ROOMMATE AT WELLESLEY, WHEN WE BOTH MOVED TO NEW YORK AND WERE STARTING TO ENTERTAIN. I OFTEN MAKE IT IN A RING MOLD AND PUT A BUNCH OF WATERCRESS IN THE CENTER. IT'S ALWAYS A CROWD-PLEASER, BUT THEN, AS MY MOTHER WOULD SAY, OF COURSE IT TASTES GOOD: IT'S MADE WITH MAYONNAISE AND SOUR CREAM!

POACHING THE SALMON FROM SCRATCH GIVES THIS TERRINE DEEPER, MORE COMPLEX FLAVOR THAN WITH CANNED SALMON. THOUGH YOU MAY PREFER TO EAT COOKED SALMON A TRIFLE UNDERDONE, LIKE MEDIUM OR EVEN MEDIUM-RARE, FOR THIS RECIPE, THE SALMON SHOULD BE COOKED THROUGH. ALLOWING IT TO COOL IN THE FUMET, OR POACHING LIQUID, ENHANCES THE FLAVOR. AND IF YOU STRAIN THE LIQUID, YOU CAN FREEZE ANY EXTRA TO USE IN OTHER RECIPES AS FISH STOCK.

There are several methods for unmolding a terrine or similar dish, including putting a hot towel over the metal mold, or dipping the mold in hot water. One of the more effective tricks is to run a hair dryer over the outside of the mold until the mold lifts off easily. Once a jellied terrine has been unmolded, it should be refrigerated, uncovered, so any softened edges can set.

6 TO 8 SERVINGS

1 CUP DRY WHITE WINE

1 LARGE ONION

2 SPRIGS FRESH THYME

2-INCH STRIP LEMON PEEL

1 POUND BONELESS SALMON, PREFERABLY CENTER-CUT FILLET

1 TABLESPOON EXTRA VIRGIN OLIVE OIL

1 PACKAGE UNFLAVORED GELATIN

3 TABLESPOONS LEMON JUICE

1 CUP MAYONNAISE

2 TABLESPOONS CHOPPED DILL, PLUS SPRIGS FOR GARNISH

1 CUP SOUR CREAM OR WHOLE MILK YOGURT

SALT AND FRESHLY GROUND WHITE PEPPER

1 ENGLISH CUCUMBER, SLICED PAPER-THIN, OPTIONAL

Bring the wine, a ½-inch-thick slice of the onion, the thyme, and the lemon peel to a simmer in a 3-quart saucepan. Add the salmon and barely simmer for 10 minutes; then turn off the heat and allow it to cool for 30 minutes.

Meanwhile, grease a 4- to 5-cup loaf pan or decorative ring mold with the olive oil. Chop the remaining onion.

Remove the salmon from the poaching liquid and drain well. Strain the poaching liquid. Place ½ cup of the poaching liquid in a small saucepan and bring to a simmer, or place it in a glass measuring cup and microwave for 1 minute. Pour the hot liquid into the bowl of a food processor and add the gelatin, chopped onion, and lemon juice. Pulse briefly just to blend the ingredients.

Add the mayonnaise and dill and pulse to blend the ingredients. Break up the salmon and add it. Pulse until the salmon is fairly finely chopped. Transfer the ingredients to a bowl and fold in the sour cream or yogurt. Season to taste with salt and pepper.

Pour the salmon mixture into the mold, cover with plastic wrap, and refrigerate at least 6 hours. Unmold. If desired, cover the top of the terrine with slightly overlapping cucumber slices, like fish scales, and garnish with dill sprigs.

NOTE: This recipe can also be made with other fish, crabmeat, or even chicken.

CASSEROLES FOR A CROWD

Creamed Artichoke-Spinach Casserole

Heirloom Scalloped Tomatoes

Summer Squash and Zucchini Casserole

Martha's Vineyard Kidney Bean Casserole

Sweet Potato and Apple Casserole

Baked Spinach Risotto

Palm Springs Chile con Queso

Mother's Macaroni and Cheese

California Chili-Rice Casserole

Cheese Grits Soufflé

Two Cheese Soufflé

Scalloped Oysters

Spanish Seafood Casserole

Coquilles St.-Jacques

Yanna's Moussaka

Left: Summer Squash and Zucchini Casserole

Creamed Artichoke–Spinach Casserole

THIS DISH IS ONE OF MY MOST DEPENDABLE, TO ROUND OUT A DINNER. THE INGREDIENTS ARE READILY AVAILABLE, AND IT'S EASILY PREPARED. IT IS ONE OF THE EARLIEST RECIPES I CAN REMEMBER PREPARING AFTER I WAS MARRIED, AND I PROBABLY GOT IT WHEN TRADING RECIPES WITH FRIENDS.

REMEMBER THE TRICK OF SQUEEZING THE MOISTURE OUT OF SPINACH BY USING A POTATO RICER. IT WORKS LIKE A CHARM. TAKE NOTE, TOO, OF THE FROZEN ARTICHOKE HEARTS—ANOTHER RELIABLE PANTRY STAPLE. THEY ARE EASILY THAWED AND USED WITHOUT COOKING, JUST MARINATED IN A VINAIGRETTE DRESSING, FOR A SALAD. AND THEY ADD A SOPHISTICATED TOUCH TO A VEGETABLE CASSEROLE.

20 TO 24 OUNCES FRESH SPINACH

1 CUP HEAVY CREAM

1 CUP GRATED GRUYÈRE, CHEDDAR, PARMIGIANO-REGGIANO, OR ASIAGO CHEESE, ABOUT 4 OUNCES

2 1/2 TABLESPOONS UNSALTED BUTTER

1 SMALL ONION, CHOPPED

4 SCALLIONS, CHOPPED

2 PACKAGES (9 OUNCES EACH) FROZEN ARTICHOKE HEARTS, THAWED

1 TABLESPOON FINELY CHOPPED DILL

4 TO 6 SERVINGS

Thoroughly rinse the spinach and remove the heavy stems. Place the spinach in a large skillet and cook until it is completely wilted. Squeeze it dry in a potato ricer or in paper towels. Chop it. Mix the spinach with the cream and half the cheese and season to taste with salt and pepper.

Preheat the oven to 350 degrees. Use ½ tablespoon of the butter to grease a 1½-quart baking dish.

Dry the skillet that you used for the spinach and melt the remaining butter in it. Add the onion and scallions and sauté until tender. Stir in the artichoke hearts and cook over medium heat, stirring, until they start to brown. Stir in the dill. Season with salt and pepper.

Spread the artichokes in the baking dish. Spread the spinach mixture on top. Sprinkle evenly with the remaining cheese. Bake about 40 minutes.

The recipe is easily doubled or tripled for a buffet table. Just be sure to bake it in a dish that is attractive enough for serving. Another option, if you have ramekins, is to bake individual portions to serve alongside a steak dinner, as an inventive version of that steakhouse staple, creamed spinach.

LAURA YAGGY

Heirloom Scalloped Tomatoes

Here is a recipe that comes from my paternal grandmother, who could not boil water but managed to serve this delicious casserole. She gave the recipe to my mother and now it's on its third generation! It's a family favorite for Easter lunch. The original recipe does not call for herbes de Provence, but they add a nicely fragrant touch to the tomatoes.

When made with canned tomatoes, this casserole can brighten a menu on a cold winter day. For an informal way to serve it, bake it in one or two large cast-iron skillets and place the skillets, with the contents bubbling from the oven, on trivets directly on your buffet table. Just be sure to wrap the handles in cloth napkins once the pans come out of the oven. The kind of bread you use will also alter the character of the dish. Whole wheat plays very nicely off the tomatoes, though white is a safe choice. Rye bread will contribute a touch of caraway seasoning. Even a rustic olive bread would be terrific.

2 cans (28 ounces each) whole plum tomatoes, drained

6 to 8 tablespoons dark brown sugar

1 teaspoon herbes de Provence

1/2 teaspoon salt, or to taste

2 tablespoons lemon juice

6 cups diced stale whole wheat, white, or rye bread,
about 1/2 pound

1/4 pound (1 stick) unsalted butter, melted

8 SERVINGS

Preheat the oven to 350 degrees.

Combine the tomatoes, sugar, herbes de Provence, salt, and lemon juice in a saucepan and simmer just until the sugar has dissolved. Add additional sugar if desired.

Toss the diced bread in the melted butter. Add half to the tomato mixture. Spread in a shallow, 2- to 3-quart baking dish. Top with the remaining bread cubes.

Place the baking dish in the oven and bake about 30 minutes, until firm.

The heirloom in the title refers to the origin of the recipe, not the kind of tomatoes used in it. But in summer, it can be made with fresh, very ripe tomatoes. Once you have peeled the tomatoes (see sidebar, page 67), quarter them, sprinkle them with salt, and let them drain in a sieve for 45 minutes (save the juice to add to soups or sauces). You will need about 18 tomatoes. And if you make the recipe with fresh tomatoes, scatter slivers of basil on the casserole just before serving.

ALEXIS WALLER

Summer Squash and Zucchini Casserole

MY GRANDMOTHER AND MY MOTHER USED TO MAKE THIS WONDERFUL SUMMER DISH ALL SEASON LONG AT OUR HOUSE IN THE MOUNTAINS OF NORTH CAROLINA. AND ALL THE INGREDIENTS CAME FRESH FROM OUR GARDEN. WHEN I WAS A CHILD, I HELPED PICK THE VEGETABLES. THE CASSEROLE WAS ALWAYS SERVED ALONGSIDE GRILLED CHICKEN, BURGERS, OR FRESHLY CAUGHT FISH, WITH CORN ON THE COB TOO. I STILL SERVE IT THE SAME WAY, AND I LOVE IT WHEN I SEE MY CHILDREN PICKING VEGETABLES FROM OUR TINY GARDEN AND THEN ENJOYING THEM. IT BRINGS BACK WARM MEMORIES OF MY OWN CHILDHOOD, AND I CHERISH THE TRADITIONS THAT CONTINUE.

There is no point in preparing this casserole unless you can obtain fresh zucchini, both green and gold, summer squash, and tomatoes. Greenmarkets, farmer's markets, and farm stands, if not your own garden, should be your sources. Select zucchini and squashes that are medium-size, no more than about 8 inches. Larger than that and they may be watery, and smaller ones can be a trifle bitter.

8 SERVINGS

3 TABLESPOONS EXTRA VIRGIN OLIVE OIL

2 LARGE SWEET ONIONS, SLICED 1/2 INCH THICK

3 LARGE RIPE BEEFSTEAK OR HEIRLOOM TOMATOES,
SLICED 1/2 INCH THICK

3 MEDIUM-SIZE ZUCCHINI, SLICED ON AN ANGLE 1/2 INCH THICK

3 MEDIUM-SIZE YELLOW SQUASH OR GOLDEN ZUCCHINI,
SLICED ON AN ANGLE 1/2 INCH THICK

2 CLOVES GARLIC, MINCED

1 TABLESPOON FRESH THYME LEAVES

1 TABLESPOON SLIVERED FRESH BASIL LEAVES

SALT AND FRESHLY GROUND BLACK PEPPER

1 1/2 POUNDS RIPE PLUM TOMATOES, PEELED AND QUARTERED
(SEE SIDEBAR, PAGE 67)

2/3 CUP SHREDDED WHITE CHEDDAR OR GRUYÈRE CHEESE,
ABOUT 3 OUNCES

Preheat the oven to 350 degrees.

Use about 1 tablespoon of the oil to grease an oblong casserole dish, 9 x 13 inches, about 3 quarts.

Layer the onions, tomatoes, zucchini, and squash in the casserole, seasoning them with garlic, thyme, basil, salt, and pepper as you go.

Pulse the plum tomatoes in a food processor until coarsely chopped. Spread them, with their juice, over the top of the vegetables. Season with salt and pepper. Sprinkle on the shredded cheese.

Bake the casserole for about 1 hour. Serve hot or at room temperature.

NOTE: The dish will take on a tangy, fresher flavor if you substitute crumbled goat cheese for the Cheddar or Gruyère.

B. D. GUERNSEY

Martha's Vineyard Kidney Bean Casserole

THIS IS ALWAYS ON OUR FAMILY'S FOURTH OF JULY MENU AT OUR HOUSE ON MARTHA'S VINEYARD. MY HUSBAND'S FAMILY HAS SUMMERED THERE FOR NEARLY 150 YEARS, AND WE NEVER MISS THE HOLIDAY CELEBRATION ON THE ISLAND. THE DISH IS AN EASY TAKE ON NEW ENGLAND BAKED BEANS. I USUALLY MAKE IT EARLY IN THE DAY AND LET IT SIT UNTIL THE EVENING. I EITHER SERVE IT AS IT IS OR REHEAT IT. AT OUR SUMMER HOUSE, THE MENU INCLUDES BAKED HAM IN THIN SLICES, PASTA SALAD, A GREEN SALAD, CORN BREAD, AND BLUEBERRY PIE. BUT THIS CASSEROLE IS TERRIFIC ON A BUFFET WITH OTHER TRADITIONAL HOLIDAY FOODS: HOT DOGS, HAMBURGERS, POTATO SALAD, COLESLAW, AND FRESH STRAWBERRIES.

THOUGH HOT DOG MUSTARD CAN BE USED IN THE CASSEROLE, GRAINY FRENCH MUSTARD ADDS A SOPHISTICATED TOUCH. THE CHILI SAUCE CALLED FOR IS THE MILD, KETCHUP-Y KIND, NOT SOME FANCY HOT SAUCE. BUT A SPLASH OF YOUR FAVORITE HOT SAUCE COULD RAMP UP THE FLAVOR VERY NICELY. ONCE THIS CASSEROLE HAS BEEN BAKED, THE BEANS CAN BE TRANSFERRED TO A SERVING BOWL. IF YOU HAVE A RUSTIC, COVERED BEAN POT, BY ALL MEANS USE IT FOR COOKING AND SERVING.

4 CANS (16 OUNCES EACH) RED KIDNEY BEANS,
DRAINED AND RINSED
½ CUP CHILI SAUCE OR KETCHUP
⅓ CUP DARK BROWN SUGAR
½ CUP GRAINY MUSTARD
1 RED ONION, FINELY CHOPPED

10 TO 12 SERVINGS

Preheat the oven to 300 degrees.

Mix the beans, chili sauce, brown sugar, mustard, and onion together in a heavy casserole.

Cover and bake for 1 hour. Serve.

If you want to prepare the beans from scratch, you will need about 1 ½ pounds dried red kidney beans or white Italian cannellini beans. Soak them overnight in a bowl, covered in cold water to a depth of 2 inches. Drain, place them in a saucepan and add fresh unsalted water, again covering the beans to a depth of 2 inches. Simmer, partly covered, until the beans are tender, about 1 hour. Do not add salt to the beans beforehand as this can prevent them from becoming properly tender.

Sweet Potato and Apple Casserole

THIS RECIPE IS A REGULAR ON OUR THANKSGIVING TABLE. I OFTEN MAKE IT WITH A LOT OF SUGAR, SO IT BECOMES A VEGETABLE THAT TASTES LIKE DESSERT, AND IT'S POPULAR WITH THOSE WHO HAVE A SWEET TOOTH. IF YOU HAVE LEFTOVERS, INSTEAD OF MERELY REHEATING AS IS, YOU CAN PULSE THEM IN A FOOD PROCESSOR UNTIL NOT QUITE A SMOOTH PUREE AND THEN REHEAT THE MIXTURE IN A SAUCEPAN OR IN A MICROWAVE OVEN TO SERVE AS A SIDE DISH.

4 SWEET POTATOES, ABOUT 2 POUNDS

3 TART APPLES

5 TABLESPOONS UNSALTED BUTTER, SOFTENED

SALT AND FRESHLY GROUND BLACK PEPPER

4 TABLESPOONS DARK BROWN SUGAR, OR MORE TO TASTE

1 TEASPOON CINNAMON

2/3 CUP APPLE CIDER

1 TABLESPOON LEMON JUICE

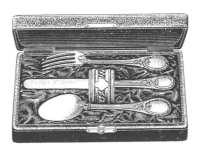

8 SERVINGS

Place the sweet potatoes in a saucepan, add water to cover them, and bring to a boil. Cook for 10 minutes; then drain and peel the potatoes. Slice the potatoes ½ inch thick.

Peel and core the apples and slice them ¼ inch thick.

Use 1 tablespoon of the butter to grease a 9-inch square baking dish.

Arrange a layer of the sweet potatoes in the dish. Season them with salt and pepper. Cover with a layer of the apples. Mix the sugar and cinnamon together and sprinkle half of it over the apples. Dot with half the remaining butter.

Repeat the layers.

Mix the cider and the lemon juice together and pour over the ingredients in the baking dish.

Preheat the oven to 375 degrees.

Cover the baking dish with foil and bake for 45 minutes. Uncover and bake another 15 to 20 minutes, until a small knife easily pierces the sweet potato. Allow to cool 10 minutes before serving.

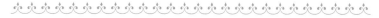

How long it takes for the potatoes to become tender will depend on their size. Try to find medium–size ones, no more than 8 ounces each, and all the same size so they cook uniformly. A type of sweet potato called Garnet is deep red and has a particularly rich flavor. The amount of sugar in the dish will depend on your taste; it can be doubled. And other ingredients, including raisins or diced dried apricots or prunes can be added, simply scattered over the layer of sweet potatoes.

Baked Spinach Risotto

I CUT A RECIPE LIKE THIS OUT OF A MAGAZINE LONG AGO, AND I HAVE MADE IT OVER AND OVER, ADDING MY OWN TOUCHES. THE GARLIC IS IMPORTANT.

I USED TO SERVE THE RISOTTO AS A SIDE DISH, BUT THEN WHEN MY DAUGHTERS WERE YOUNG, IT BECAME A MAIN DISH BECAUSE IT WAS MADE WITH INGREDIENTS THEY LOVE AND WERE WILLING TO EAT. THEY WOULD NOT TOUCH PLAIN SPINACH, BUT THIS WAY THEY WOULD CLEAN THEIR PLATES. I ALSO LOVE THE FACT THAT THE CASSEROLE FREEZES WELL. I CAN TAKE IT TO OUR COUNTRY HOUSE FOR FRIDAY NIGHT SUPPER ON THE WEEKEND, AND I HAVE EVEN BROUGHT IT WHEN I WAS A WEEKEND GUEST. AND OF COURSE, IT'S PERFECT FOR A POTLUCK SUPPER.

2$\frac{1}{2}$ TABLESPOONS EXTRA VIRGIN OLIVE OIL

2 CUPS CHOPPED ONION

4 CLOVES GARLIC, MINCED

2$\frac{1}{4}$ CUPS ARBORIO RICE

1$\frac{1}{2}$ CUPS DRY WHITE WINE

4$\frac{1}{2}$ CUPS VEGETABLE STOCK

1 BAG (10 OUNCES) SPINACH, RINSED, HEAVY STEMS REMOVED, CHOPPED

1 CUP GRATED PARMIGIANO-REGGIANO, ABOUT 4 OUNCES

1 TEASPOON SALT

FRESHLY GROUND BLACK PEPPER TO TASTE

10 TO 12 SERVINGS

Preheat the oven to 375 degrees. Grease a 9 x 13-inch baking dish with ½ tablespoon of the oil.

Heat the remaining oil in a large sauté pan over medium heat. Add the onions and garlic and cook until soft, about 5 minutes. Add the rice and stir well. Cook for 2 minutes. Add the wine and cook, stirring, until the wine is absorbed. Stir in the stock and bring to a boil. Reduce the heat to low and simmer 6 to 8 minutes. Stir in the spinach, ½ cup of the cheese, the salt, and pepper.

Spoon the mixture into the baking dish. Sprinkle with the remaining cheese. Cover with foil and bake 30 minutes.

NOTE: Baking short-grain Arborio rice is unusual but the grains swell nicely and have the creamy texture that you want from a risotto.

A lovely addition to bolster this casserole and turn it into a one-dish supper would be sliced hard-cooked eggs. Spoon half the spinach and rice mixture into the casserole, add the sliced eggs, then top with the remaining mixture and the cheese. Slices of cooked chicken, sausages, or ham can also be used in the same fashion.

Palm Springs Chile con Queso

I WAS BORN AND RAISED IN PALM SPRINGS, CALIFORNIA. OUR LIVES REVOLVED AROUND THE OUTDOORS, SO MY MOTHER DID NOT SPEND A LOT OF TIME COOKING. THIS WAS ONE OF HER RECIPES, EASY AND FOOLPROOF. IT ALSO HAS A MEXICAN ACCENT, WHICH WE LOVE. CANNED GREEN CHILIES ARE A WONDERFUL EMERGENCY INGREDIENT TO KEEP ON THE PANTRY SHELF. AND WITH SOME CHEESE, EGGS, AND MILK, ALL REFRIGERATOR STAPLES, YOU HAVE AN IMPRESSIVE, LAST-MINUTE DISH. YOU CAN VARY THE CHEESES AND MIX THE CHILIES WITH OTHER INGREDIENTS LIKE MINCED SCALLIONS OR ONIONS, DICED TOMATO, OR EVEN RAISINS.

½ TABLESPOON UNSALTED BUTTER, SOFTENED

4 CANS (4 OUNCES EACH) CHOPPED GREEN CHILIES

1½ CUPS COOKED CHICKEN OR TURKEY, SHREDDED, OR ½ POUND BACON, COOKED AND CRUMBLED, OPTIONAL

2 CUPS GRATED SHARP WHITE CHEDDAR CHEESE, ABOUT 8 OUNCES

2 CUPS GRATED MONTEREY JACK CHEESE, ABOUT 8 OUNCES

8 EGGS

1 CUP MILK

½ TEASPOON GROUND CUMIN

Preheat the oven to 350 degrees. Butter an oblong baking dish, 9 x 13 inches.

Spread the chilies in the baking dish.

If you are using the optional chicken, turkey, or bacon, scatter it over the chilies.

Cover with the cheeses. Beat the eggs and the milk together. Beat in the cumin. Pour this mixture over the cheese. Bake 30 to 40 minutes, until lightly browned on top.

Allow to sit 10 minutes, then cut into squares and serve.

This casserole makes twelve servings for a buffet or, with a green salad alongside, for lunch or supper; it can also be cut into small squares, yielding four dozen appetizer tidbits. But as an hors d'oeuvre, it should be made just with cheeses, no meat. Another way to prepare it is to use the mixture as a filling for two 9-inch pie or tart shells (see recipe, page 217), making it into a chili quiche con queso. With the meat, it makes for an excellent brunch dish, served with a bowl of sour cream alongside. Consider using diced cooked ham or purchased duck confit, shredded, as alternatives for the meat. This dish is so versatile, it can be made in advance and reheated, even for breakfast the next morning!

Mother's Macaroni and Cheese

MY LITTLE BROTHER AND I LOVED "MAC AND CHEESE" WHEN WE WERE GROWING UP. MY MOTHER, CARLA MACMILLAN, SERVED IT AT EVERY SPECIAL OCCASION OF OUR YOUNG LIVES, LIKE THE NIGHT BEFORE WE WENT TO SLEEP-AWAY CAMP, THE LAST DAY OF SCHOOL, FOR BIRTHDAYS, AND FOR JUST ABOUT EVERY OTHER CELEBRATION. SHE REFUSED TO BUY BOXED MACARONI AND CHEESE MIX AND CLAIMED HER VERSION WAS MORE AUTHENTIC AND MUCH HEALTHIER. AS A CHILD I LIKED MILD CHEDDAR AND SWISS CHEESE, BUT AS AN ADULT, I PREFER RICHER CHEESES LIKE GRUYÈRE. FEED IT TO CHILDREN AND THEY WILL NEVER WANT THE "BOXED STUFF" AGAIN!

7 TABLESPOONS UNSALTED BUTTER

2 TABLESPOONS DRY MUSTARD

6 TABLESPOONS FLOUR

3 CUPS MILK

6 CUPS SHREDDED CHEDDAR CHEESE OR A MIXTURE OF CHEESES,
ABOUT 1 1/2 POUNDS

1 POUND ELBOW MACARONI

SALT AND FRESHLY GROUND BLACK PEPPER

The most important thing to remember when you are planning to serve this dish to children is that grownups will want to have some. And if you plan to serve it to a family crowd or just to adults, be sure to prepare an ample quantity. You cannot underestimate how much your guests, especially the men, but even the chic, carb-conscious ladies, will wind up eating. Any leftovers, of course, can always be reheated.

6 TO 8 SERVINGS

In a 3-quart saucepan, melt 6
tablespoons of the butter. Whisk the
mustard and flour together, add to the
butter, and stir with a wooden spoon.
Gradually stir in the milk. Cook,
whisking over medium heat, until the
sauce thickens. Stir in the cheese.
Season to taste with salt and pepper and
set aside, covered.

Bring a large pot of water to a boil.
Add the macaroni and cook until al
dente, about 6 minutes. Drain the pasta,
transfer to a large bowl, and pour the
cheese sauce over it. Fold the two
together. Season to taste with salt and
pepper.

Preheat the oven to 350 degrees.
Grease a 4-quart baking dish with the
remaining butter. Spoon the macaroni
and cheese into the dish and bake about

30 minutes or until the edges are bubbling and the casserole is starting to brown.
Serve while hot.

NOTE: This version of macaroni and cheese is as basic as it gets. But it can become
a platform for variations, like a topping of buttered bread crumbs or the addition of
diced ham. Even other macaroni shapes, like shells or penne, can be used.

California Chili-Rice Casserole

This is one of my mother's recipes, and she included it in *The California Heritage Cookbook* for the Pasadena Junior League, which she helped to create in the 1970s. We used to live in Southern California, and my mother was a big fan of Mexican food. She could easily find the ingredients, and she even gave Mexican-themed dinner parties. You can adjust the spiciness with more chilies or less. And it looks great in a fun and colorful ceramic dish.

I cup long grain rice

Salt

I cup sour cream

2 cups grated Monterey Jack or other cheese,
about 8 ounces

2 1/2 tablespoons unsalted butter

I can (4 ounces) diced green chilies, drained

1/2 cup grated Parmigiano-Reggiano

6 SERVINGS

Bring 2 cups of water to a boil in a 2-quart saucepan; stir in the rice and ½ teaspoon salt. Reduce the heat to low. Cover the pan and cook about 20 minutes, until the water is absorbed and the rice is tender. Set the rice aside, covered, for 10 minutes. Uncover, transfer the rice to a bowl, fluff with a fork, and allow to cool to room temperature.

Mix the rice with the sour cream and grated Monterey Jack. Season to taste with salt.

Preheat the oven to 350 degrees. Grease an 8-inch square baking dish with ½ tablespoon of the butter.

Spread half the rice mixture in the dish. Spread chilies on top. Cover with the remaining cheese. Dot with the remaining butter and dust with the Parmigiano-Reggiano. Bake about 30 minutes and then serve.

The spiciness of the chilies gives this dish its kick, to it's best to use a mild cheese, like Monterey Jack. It can become a more substantial dish, a main course, if you add slices of cooked chicken, pieces of cooked shrimp, slices of chorizo, or crumbled cooked sausage meat along with the chilies. This casserole can easily be made in advance and reheated, so it's perfect for effortless entertaining or to bring to a potluck supper.

LAURA YAGGY

Cheese Grits Soufflé

My brother married a Southern girl, and she was spending Christmas with our family for the first time. My mother thought it would be fun to honor her roots with a dish at Christmas eve. She came up with this recipe, which has become a family staple.

Stone-ground grits are the best kind to buy. They have better texture and flavor, and more nutrients. You can vary the kind of cheese in this recipe, using Gruyère, Parmigiano-Reggiano or Manchego to give the dish a slightly different flavor personality.

¼ pound (1 stick) unsalted butter

1½ cups grated sharp white Cheddar cheese,
about 6 ounces

4 cups milk

1 teaspoon salt

1 cup stone-ground grits

1 tablespoon freshly ground black pepper, or to taste

Cayenne, to taste

4 large eggs, separated

6 to 8 servings

Preheat the oven to 375 degrees. Use ½ tablespoon of the butter to grease a 2-quart soufflé dish. Dust the dish with a little of the cheese.

Heat the milk to a simmer in a heavy saucepan with the salt. Gradually pour in the grits—use a measuring cup with a spout—and whisk constantly to blend them in. Cook, stirring, about 30 minutes, until the grits leave the sides of the pan. Fold in the remaining butter and cheese and season to taste with pepper, cayenne, and salt, if needed. Remove from the heat.

Beat the egg yolks until blended and gradually fold into the grits mixture.

Beat the whites until they are stiff enough to hold peaks but still look creamy. Fold the whites into the grits mixture. Pour into the soufflé dish and bake for about 40 minutes, until the soufflé is puffed and golden brown.

Serve at once.

There is nothing like a classic straight-sided fluted French soufflé dish—form meets function—for a recipe like this, even one that has no European accent whatsoever. The straight sides encourage the soufflé to rise and the dusting of cheese around the inside of the dish gives the mixture something to "grab" as it rises. Other recipes might use bread crumbs or sugar for this purpose. Making family-style serving even easier, the white porcelain is always elegant on the table. But to give your presentation a more down-home look, wrap a checked napkin or even a cotton bandana around the dish before you bring it to the table.

Two Cheese Soufflé

Some husbands do all the grilling, but mine makes soufflés. It's fine with me. This cheese soufflé, made with cubes of cheese for an interesting twist on the classic, is one of his specialties. We like to serve it for a Sunday supper with stewed tomatoes and a green salad.

3½ tablespoons unsalted butter, softened

¾ cup grated Parmigiano-Reggiano, about 3 ounces

3 tablespoons flour

1 cup milk

4 large eggs, separated

1 whole egg

Salt and freshly ground black pepper

Pinch of cayenne pepper

1 tablespoon Dijon-style mustard

3 ounces Gruyère cheese, cut in small cubes

Pinch of cream of tartar

4 SERVINGS

Preheat the oven to 425 degrees.

Prepare a 1½-quart soufflé dish by brushing it with ½ tablespoon of the butter and dusting it with ¼ cup of the grated Parmigiano-Reggiano. Refrigerate until needed.

Melt the remaining butter in a medium, heavy pan. Add the flour; stir to mix and cook for 3 to 4 minutes over low heat, whisking, until golden brown. Off the heat, pour in the milk all at once and whisk until smooth. Return to the heat and cook, stirring, until the sauce has thickened.

Off the heat, beat in the egg yolks one at a time, stirring vigorously after each addition. Beat in the whole egg. Add the salt, pepper, and cayenne to taste. Stir in the mustard and the remaining grated Parmigiano-Reggiano.

Beat the egg whites until they foam. Add a pinch of cream of tartar and continue beating until they hold definite peaks but still look creamy.

Stir the cubed Gruyère into the egg yolk and cheese base, and then quickly fold in the egg whites before the cubes of Gruyère have time to melt.

Spoon the soufflé mixture into the prepared dish. Place in the oven and immediately reduce the temperature to 400 degrees. Bake for 25 minutes in the middle of the oven, until the soufflé is puffed and golden. Serve at once.

Though this soufflé, like most, demands all your attention the minute it comes out of the oven—waiting and cooling will cause it to sink—the fact that most of the preparation can be done in advance (and you have the baking time to complete the other tasks for the dinner) makes it a convenient dish to serve. You do have to be organized. The soufflé can even replace the cheese course at a formal dinner. Plan on having the other components of the meal ready, and serve a first course, if you wish, the moment the soufflé goes into the oven. Then all you have to do is clear, bring out the soufflé, and take a bow!

GRACE MEIGHER

Scalloped Oysters

THESE SCALLOPED OYSTERS HAVE BEEN A FAMILY FAVORITE FOR AS LONG AS I CAN REMEMBER. AS A LITTLE GIRL, I COULDN'T STAND THE SIGHT AND SMELL OF RAW OYSTERS AND WOULD NOT EVEN GO NEAR THIS DISH UNTIL I WAS MARRIED. MY HUSBAND THOUGHT IT WAS FABULOUS, SO I DECIDED TO TRY IT AT A FAMILY HOLIDAY DINNER. (IT WAS ALWAYS SERVED AT THANKSGIVING, FOR EXAMPLE.) TO MY SURPRISE, I FOUND IT TO BE DELICIOUS, SO NOW, IN OUR HOUSE, A FAMILY TRADITION LIVES ON.

WHETHER THIS OYSTER CASSEROLE GOES ON A BUFFET, OR IS SERVED AS A FIRST COURSE OR A MAIN COURSE FOR A SUPPER, IT DESERVES AN ELEGANT PRESENTATION, SUCH AS A GLASS DISH SET IN ITS OWN SILVER CARRIER, OR A PORCELAIN BAKING DISH ON A SILVER TRAY.

I QUART SHUCKED OYSTERS, WITH THEIR LIQUOR
(ABOUT 6 DOZEN OYSTERS)

½ CUP SEAFOOD STOCK OR CLAM JUICE, APPROXIMATELY

¼ POUND (I STICK) UNSALTED BUTTER

4 CUPS CRUSHED OYSTER CRACKERS (ABOUT IO OUNCES)

SALT AND FRESHLY GROUND BLACK PEPPER

2 CUPS HALF-AND-HALF

CAYENNE, TO TASTE

8 SERVINGS

Drain the oysters, reserving the liquor, and remove any bits of shell. Measure the liquor and add enough seafood stock or clam juice to make ¾ cup. Set aside.

Use some of the butter to grease a shallow 3-quart casserole. Spread one-third of the cracker crumbs in the casserole and cover with half the oysters. Dot with 2½ tablespoons of the butter and sprinkle with salt and pepper. Repeat the layers.

Top with the remaining cracker crumbs and dot with the remaining butter.

Preheat the oven to 400 degrees.

Combine the half-and-half with the reserved oyster liquid and stir well. Season with the cayenne. Pour over the top of the casserole.

Place in the oven, immediately reduce the heat to 350 degrees, and bake for 30 minutes or until set.

NOTE: The easiest way to crush the crackers is to put them in a plastic bag and go over the bag with a rolling pin or the bottom of a saucepan.

If you are expert at opening oysters, go right ahead and shuck them for this recipe. But it is far easier to buy or to order shucked oysters from a fish market. Be sure to reserve every precious drop of the liquid, called liquor, that comes with the oysters.

Coquilles St.–Jacques

I DON'T KNOW WHEN I GOT THIS RECIPE. IT WAS AGES AGO. AND THE WOMAN WHO GAVE IT TO ME SAID TO MAKE IT WITH CRABMEAT, WHICH IS WHAT I HAVE ALWAYS DONE. THE DISH IS A REAL CROWD-PLEASER AT ALL OF MY PARTIES. I ESPECIALLY LIKE TO SERVE IT IN THE SHELLS BECAUSE IT MAKES FOR A BEAUTIFUL PRESENTATION. STORES THAT SELL COOKWARE AND TABLE UTENSILS OFTEN HAVE REAL FLUTED SHELLS THAT HAVE BEEN CLEANED AND STERILIZED AND CAN BE USED FOR BAKING AND SERVING A DISH LIKE THIS.

2 TABLESPOONS UNSALTED BUTTER

1/2 CUP SOFT FRESH BREAD CRUMBS OR PANKO (SEE NOTE)

1/2 POUND SEA SCALLOPS, DICED

1/2 CUP MAYONNAISE

1/3 CUP MILK

3 HARD-COOKED EGGS, FINELY CHOPPED

1/3 CUP FINELY CHOPPED ONION

SALT AND FRESHLY GROUND BLACK PEPPER

2 TABLESPOONS MINCED CHIVES

Preheat the oven to 350 degrees. Use some of the butter to grease a 1-quart baking dish or 6 ramekins or large scallop shells.

Melt the remaining butter in a small pan, add bread crumbs and cook, stirring, about 5 minutes, until golden. Set aside.

Combine the scallops, mayonnaise, milk, eggs, and onions in a bowl. Season to taste with salt and pepper. Pile the mixture into baking dish or individual dishes and top with buttered crumbs. Place in the oven and bake 20 to 25 minutes, until heated through and lightly browned on top.

Dust with chives and serve.

NOTE: Panko is the name for dried, untoasted Japanese bread crumbs. They are fairly widely sold now. Their texture is coarser than commercial American bread crumbs.

Sea scallops—the creatures that are called coquilles St.-Jacques in French—often have a tough little strip of tendon on the side. Remove it before using the scallops. Though the name of the recipe insists on scallops, other seafood, including lump crabmeat, diced lobster, tiny shrimp, or steamed and shucked mussels will marry well with the sauce.

Spanish Seafood Casserole

THIS DISH IS PERFECT COMFORT FOOD ON A COLD EVENING. I FIRST TASTED IT IN BEDFORD, NEW YORK, WHERE WE LIVE, RIGHT AFTER OUR THIRD CHILD WAS BORN. IT WAS DELIVERED TO OUR DOOR BY FRIENDS. BEDFORD IS A CLOSE-KNIT COMMUNITY, WHERE EVERYONE SPRINGS INTO ACTION FOR THOSE WHO NEED A LITTLE HELP, ESPECIALLY IF THERE IS A BIRTH, AN ILLNESS, OR DEATH IN THE FAMILY. I OFTEN PREPARE IT EARLY IN THE DAY, PUT IT IN THE REFRIGERATOR, AND THEN LET IT COOK JUST BEFORE DINNER.

2 TABLESPOONS EXTRA VIRGIN OLIVE OIL

1 LARGE ONION, FINELY CHOPPED

½ CUP CHOPPED GREEN PEPPER

4 CLOVES GARLIC, MINCED

2 CUPS RICE, PREFERABLY SPANISH SHORT GRAIN

2 TEASPOONS PAPRIKA, PREFERABLY SPANISH

6 CUPS CHICKEN STOCK

SALT AND FRESHLY GROUND BLACK PEPPER

2 POUNDS COOKED LOBSTER MEAT (IN 1-INCH CHUNKS; SEE NOTE, PAGE 83), COOKED SHRIMP, OR A COMBINATION

3 TABLESPOONS UNSALTED BUTTER

3 TABLESPOONS FLOUR

1 CUP HEAVY CREAM

¼ CUP DRY SHERRY

1 TABLESPOON LEMON JUICE

CAYENNE, TO TASTE

¼ CUP SLIVERED ROASTED RED PEPPERS, PREFERABLY PIQUILLO

½ CUP CHOPPED MARCONA ALMONDS

8 TO 10 SERVINGS

Heat the oil in a 3-quart saucepan. Add the onion, green pepper, and garlic and sauté over low heat until translucent. Stir in the rice and paprika. Add 4 cups of the chicken stock, stir, season with salt and pepper, and cover. Cook about 15 minutes, until almost all the stock has been absorbed and the rice is nearly tender. Set aside, covered, for 10 minutes.

Fold the lobster into the rice. Spread this mixture in a 3-quart baking dish about 10 x 13 inches.

Melt the butter in a saucepan. Whisk in the flour, and then the remaining chicken stock. Simmer, whisking, until the mixture thickens. Stir in the cream, sherry, and lemon juice. Season the sauce with salt, pepper, and cayenne.

Scatter the roasted peppers over the rice mixture and spread the sauce on top. Sprinkle with the almonds.

Preheat the oven to 350 degrees. Bake about 35 minutes, until the casserole is bubbling and the top is starting to brown.

This dish had a Spanish accent from the start, with its peppers, sherry, and almonds. Using short grain rice, adding richly smoked Spanish paprika, imported roasted piquillo peppers, and plump marcona almonds, all of which are now sold at fancy food shops and online, just makes the accent stronger. Some diced Spanish chorizo sausage can also be added to the rice and lobster mixture. For a Spanish dinner, serve cheeses, olives, and cured ham with cocktails, a salad dressed with Spanish olive oil and sherry vinegar, and flan for dessert.

Yanna's Moussaka

T HIS IS THE GREEK VERSION OF LASAGNA, SO IT'S A MAIN DISH. FOR LUNCHEON IN THE SUMMER, START WITH SOME LARGE BLACK OLIVES, HUMMUS, AND TOASTED PITA TRIANGLES, AND THEN SERVE THE MOUSSAKA WITH A SALAD AND A LOAF OF GOOD, FRESH BREAD. FOR DESSERT, PLAN ON SOMETHING LIGHT, SUCH AS FRESH BERRIES, TROPICAL SORBETS, AND TINY LEMON COOKIES. THIS RECIPE COMES FROM YANNA, OUR FAMILY'S FORMER HOUSEKEEPER, AND IT IS THE BEST MOUSSAKA THAT I HAVE EVER TASTED. BY THE WAY, IT'S PRONOUNCED "MOOSE-SOCK-AHHH" WITH THE EMPHASIS ON THE "AHHH," AND IT TOOK MUCH BEGGING ON MY PART TO GET YANNA TO GIVE ME THE RECIPE. TRY TO BUY THE INGREDIENTS THE DAY BEFORE OR YOU WILL BE PRESSED FOR TIME. YOU WILL NEED A BIG, DEEP CASSEROLE DISH THAT CAN GO FROM OVEN TO TABLE.

1 1/2 POUNDS EGGPLANTS, IN SLICES 3/8 INCH THICK

SALT

1/2 CUP EXTRA VIRGIN OLIVE OIL

1 LARGE ONION, FINELY CHOPPED

3 LARGE CLOVES GARLIC, FINELY CHOPPED

2 POUNDS GROUND BEEF OR LAMB

1 CUP TOMATO PUREE

FRESHLY GROUND BLACK PEPPER

1 BAY LEAF

1 CINNAMON STICK

1/4 CUP FINELY CHOPPED FLAT-LEAF PARSLEY LEAVES

1/4 CUP FRESH MINT LEAVES

1 TEASPOON DRIED OREGANO, PREFERABLY GREEK

1 LARGE BAKING POTATO, PEELED AND SLICED 1/4 INCH THICK

4 TABLESPOONS UNSALTED BUTTER

6 TABLESPOONS FLOUR

6 TO 8 SERVINGS

3 CUPS MILK

½ TEASPOON NUTMEG

½ CUP GRATED PARMIGIANO-REGGIANO

4 LARGE EGGS, BEATEN

Spread the eggplant slices on a large cutting board and lightly salt both sides. Let them sit for at least half an hour. Heat 3 tablespoons of the oil in a 4-quart saucepan. Add the onion and garlic and sauté over low heat until they are translucent. Add the ground meat and cook, stirring constantly to break it up, until it is no longer pink. Add the tomato puree, salt and pepper to taste, the bay leaf, and the cinnamon stick. Simmer the mixture slowly for at least half an hour. Fold in the parsley, mint, and oregano. Set aside.

Preheat a broiler. Line a baking sheet with foil. Rinse the eggplant slices and drain and pat them dry. Arrange them on the baking sheet, brush them on each side, using about 4 tablespoons of the oil. Broil until they are lightly browned. Set aside.

Heat the remaining oil in a skillet and lightly brown the potato slices. Season them with salt and pepper.

Arrange the potato slices, slightly overlapping, in a large oblong casserole dish about 10 x 14 inches and at least 2 inches deep. Remove the cinnamon stick and bay leaf from the meat mixture, adjust the seasoning if necessary, and spread the meat over the potatoes. Arrange the eggplant slices, slightly overlapping, on the meat.

Place the butter in a heavy 3-quart saucepan over medium heat. When it melts, whisk in the flour. Gradually whisk in the milk. Add the nutmeg and 2 tablespoons of the Parmigiano-Reggiano. The mixture should thicken at this point, and when it does, take it off the stove and let it cool to room temperature, stirring from time to time to prevent a skin from forming. Preheat the oven to 375 degrees.

Stir the beaten eggs and 4 tablespoons of the cheese into the sauce mixture. Pour this over the eggplant and sprinkle with the remaining cheese.

Place the baking dish in the oven and cook about 45 minutes, until the top is golden brown and the moussaka is heated through. Let the moussaka rest for several minutes before serving. It can also be allowed to cool, then reheated.

THE MAIN COURSE: SEAFOOD

Accademia Lemon Spaghetti with Shrimp

Spaghetti alle Vongole

Mark's Grilled Shrimp

Scampi Buzara

Sea Bass on the Grill

Baked Halibut Jardinière

Salt-Crusted Snapper from Barcelona

Lemony Stuffed Sole Fillets

Santa Barbara Seafood Stew

Left: Scampi Buzara

BARBARA GIMBEL

Accademia Lemon Spaghetti with Shrimp

This is an authentic Italian dish—from Italy. I first enjoyed it at a lunch at the American Academy in Rome with the director, Adele Chatfield-Taylor. She served it as a main course, following a salad. I got the recipe and started serving it in our home in Todi, in Umbria, where it's a first course, with grilled chicken or grilled guinea hen and a salad afterwards.

In New York, I often make it with rock shrimp, and I only add the zucchini when it is freshest, in summer. Rock shrimp are great because they are sold peeled and require less work than regular shrimp. Plus in this recipe, their small size melds better with the pasta. I love this recipe because it is such a lovely change from all the usual tomato-based spaghetti sauces.

1 tablespoon extra virgin olive oil

½ pound small shrimp, shelled, deveined, and cut in half,
or rock shrimp, whole

1 small zucchini, trimmed and cut in julienne

Salt and freshly ground white pepper

¾ cup heavy cream

Grated zest and juice of ½ lemon

½ pound spaghetti

¼ cup vodka

4 SERVINGS

Heat the oil in a 12-inch skillet over medium heat. Add the shrimp and zucchini, season them with salt and pepper, reduce the heat to low and cook, stirring, about 5 minutes, just until the shrimp turn pink. Add the cream and lemon zest, bring everything to a simmer, and turn off the heat.

Bring a large pot of salted water to a boil for the spaghetti, cook the spaghetti until it is al dente, about 7 minutes, then drain it, reserving about ½ cup of the cooking water.

Place the spaghetti in the skillet with the cream, shrimp, and zucchini. Add the lemon juice and vodka. Cook over medium-high heat, mixing spaghetti in the cream about 5 minutes, until the cream has thickened slightly and the mixture is less soupy. Taste, and season with salt and pepper.

Divide the spaghetti, shrimp, and zucchini among 4 shallow soup plates, spooning cream from the pan over each serving. If the cream has reduced too much, you can add a little of the reserved pasta water to enhance the liquid. Serve at once.

This is a particularly light and elegant pasta but with enough richness that a moderately sized portion is more than enough. It will not embarrass your best silver and dinnerware, though it is also ideal for a luncheon, even one on a terrace in summer. It is best as a separate course dished up in the kitchen, into warm soup plates, instead of being served in a big bowl at the table or on a buffet.

Spaghetti alle Vongole

THIS IS ONE OF MY DAD'S RECIPES. HE DIVIDES HIS TIME BETWEEN NEW YORK CITY AND MILLBROOK, IN THE HUDSON VALLEY, AND WHEREVER HE IS, HE COOKS UP A STORM. HE TRIES NEW RECIPES ALL THE TIME. I REMEMBER HAVING FAIRLY EXOTIC TASTES FOR A CHILD. I LOVED ESCARGOTS, AND OF COURSE I WAS NOT DAUNTED BY SPAGHETTI WITH CLAMS. THIS RECIPE IS SIMPLE, BASIC, AND VERY AUTHENTIC.

IN ITALY, PASTA WITH CLAMS IS USUALLY SERVED WITHOUT GRATED CHEESE. BUT HAVE SOME ON HAND, IN CASE A GUEST REQUESTS IT, EVEN IF YOU MIGHT THINK IT'S A MISTAKE. THIS IS NOT A DISH FOR A BUFFET OR A CROWD, OR TO BRING TO A POTLUCK AFFAIR. IT IS STRICTLY ONE TO SERVE AT THE TABLE THE MINUTE IT IS READY. JUST BE SURE TO PROVIDE BOWLS FOR THE DISCARDED SHELLS.

3 DOZEN LITTLENECK CLAMS

SALT

1 POUND THIN SPAGHETTI OR LINGUINE

5 TABLESPOONS EXTRA VIRGIN OLIVE OIL

5 LARGE CLOVES GARLIC, CHOPPED

1 CUP CLAM JUICE, FRESH OR BOTTLED, APPROXIMATELY

3 TABLESPOONS MINCED FLAT-LEAF PARSLEY LEAVES

DRIED CHILI FLAKES TO TASTE

4 TO 6 SERVINGS

Scrub the clams shells with a stiff brush. Set aside.

Bring a large pot of salted water to a boil for the spaghetti. You will add the spaghetti when the water comes to a boil.

Meanwhile, heat 3 tablespoons of the oil in a skillet or sauté pan with a cover that is large enough to hold the clams and the pasta. Add the garlic and sauté briefly over low heat. Add the clams, cover the pan, and cook over medium heat, shaking the pan once or twice, until the clams have opened.

When the pasta is al dente, drain it and add it to the pan with the clams. Add half the clam juice, allow it to heat through, then remove the pan from the heat and use tongs or a large spoon and fork to turn the pasta in the clam mixture and combine all the ingredients. Return the pan to the heat and add as much additional clam juice as needed to make the mixture quite moist.

Pour on the remaining olive oil and sprinkle parsley over the top. Bring the pan directly to the table for serving, or transfer the contents of the pan to a large, wide, warm serving bowl and then sprinkle with the parsley. Serve at once, with dried chili flakes for guests to add at the table, to taste.

Bottled clam juice is an acceptable ingredient, though if you are lucky enough to have a fish market that sells its own frozen clam juice, by all means buy it. And if you know how to open clams and ever serve them on the half shell, do it over a bowl to catch the juice, which you can freeze, adding to the container each time you shuck clams and eventually accumulating a cup or more.

Mark's Grilled Shrimp

Our oldest son and I cook together as often as we can, usually over holidays. He has become the real cook in the family. I got this recipe from him. It's a delicious main dish, but Mark often makes this shrimp as an appetizer when we have guests, and even when we don't.

Juice of 6 limes

Juice of 3 oranges

1/2 cup soy sauce

2 jalapeño peppers, seeded and finely diced

1/3 cup minced fresh ginger

1/3 cup minced cilantro leaves, plus sprigs for garnish

Salt and freshly ground black pepper, to taste

1/2 cup extra virgin olive oil

3 pounds (about 30) jumbo shrimp, peeled and deveined, with tails left on

6 SERVINGS

Mix the lime juice, orange juice, soy sauce, jalapeños, ginger, and cilantro together in a large bowl. Season to taste with salt and pepper. Whisk in olive oil. Reserve ⅔ cup of this mixture in a glass measuring cup.

Place the shrimp in the bowl, turn them to coat with the marinade, cover, and set aside at room temperature for 30 minutes.

Heat a grill.

Grill the shrimp for 3 to 5 minutes, turning them once and basting with the marinade. You can either set the shrimp directly on the grill, use a perforated grill pan, or even place them on skewers.

Remove the shrimp to a platter. Microwave the reserved marinade for 1 minute to warm it and then pour it over the shrimp. Garnish the platter with cilantro and serve.

NOTE: If you do not have a grill, you can cook the shrimp on top of the stove in a ridged grill pan, or you can broil them.

Instead of using jumbo shrimp, the recipe can be made as a cocktail hors d'oeuvre with medium shrimp; 3 pounds of them will yield about 100. The best way to cook them is to line a jelly-roll pan with foil, place the marinated shrimp on it close together in a single layer, and broil them without turning. Then pile them on a platter with toothpicks for skewering.

HEDVIG HRICAK, M.D.

Scampi Buzara

THIS RECIPE COMES FROM MY FAMILY IN CROATIA, AND IT GOES BACK AS FAR AS MY GRANDMOTHER, WITH UPDATES OVER TIME. NOW MY SON, WHO LIVES IN SAN FRANCISCO, HAS STARTED MAKING THE SCAMPI DISH, WHICH HAS ALWAYS BEEN A FAMILY FAVORITE.

WITH SEAFOOD IN THE SHELL, THIS IS A MESSY DISH TO EAT. SLITTING THE SHELLS OR CUTTING THE SHRIMP IN HALF MAKES IT EASIER TO EXTRACT THE MEAT. STILL, IT'S A GOOD IDEA TO PROVIDE SMALL COCKTAIL FORKS IN ADDITION TO REGULAR FORKS, KNIVES, AND SOUP SPOONS OR SAUCE SPOONS. THIS DISH DEMANDS A GREAT DEAL OF FLATWARE!

24 JUMBO SHRIMP, TIGER PRAWNS OR TRUE SCAMPI (LANGOUSTINE TAILS), ABOUT 3 POUNDS

¼ CUP DRY BREAD CRUMBS

½ CUP EXTRA VIRGIN OLIVE OIL

6 LARGE CLOVES GARLIC, SLICED THIN

2 CUPS PEELED, SEEDED, CHOPPED RIPE TOMATOES (SEE SIDEBAR, PAGE 67)

2 BAY LEAVES

2 CUPS DRY WHITE WINE

SALT AND FRESHLY GROUND BLACK PEPPER

½ CUP FINELY CHOPPED FLAT-LEAF PARSLEY LEAVES

CRUSTY BREAD FOR SERVING

6 SERVINGS

If you are using shrimp or tiger prawns, they should be headless but in the shell. Use a sharp knife to cut each in half lengthwise. Langoustines, also in the shell, should be trimmed of heads, torsos, and claws, so there are only the tails where the meat is. Use kitchen shears or a sharp knife to slit the soft undersides of the langoustine tail shells, but do not cut into the meat.

Place the bread crumbs in a skillet large enough to hold all the shrimp or langoustines. Cook, stirring, over medium heat to toast them. Remove them from the pan and set aside. Wipe the pan clean.

Heat the oil in the skillet. Add garlic and sauté over medium heat until it starts to turn fragrant and golden.

Add the tomatoes and the bay leaves and simmer over low heat for 10 minutes. Add the shrimp or langoustines, and use tongs to turn them in the tomato mixture until the shells turn pink, about 3 minutes. Add the wine, salt, and pepper and bring to a fast simmer. Use tongs or a slotted spoon to remove the shrimp or langoustines to a bowl. Continue cooking the tomato mixture until about half the wine has evaporated. Check the seasonings, adding more salt and pepper if needed.

Mix in the bread crumbs, return the shrimp or langoustines to the pan, cover, and cook another 2 minutes or so.

Remove the pan from the heat, sprinkle with parsley, and divide everything among 6 shallow soup plates. Serve, with crusty bread, and bowls on the table for the discarded shells.

True scampi, which the French call langoustines and which are also known as Dublin Bay prawns, are not shrimp. They look a bit like mini-lobsters, with long, slender claws and fairly hard shells. Only the tail meat is eaten. They must be very, very fresh or their texture is likely to be mushy. To find them, you have to shop at a fairly elite market that gets them live, usually from Australia or Scotland. They are sometimes sold online, frozen, and in that form are pretty good. But do not buy them in a market where they have already been thawed. Jumbo shrimp or tiger prawns make fine substitutes.

Sea Bass on the Grill

W**E LOVE FISH ON THE GRILL IN SUMMER. WE HAVE A SUMMER HOUSE IN EAST HAMPTON, ON LONG ISLAND, A SEASIDE COMMUNITY, AND IT'S EASY TO BUY THE FRESHEST JUST-CAUGHT FISH. THERE IS NOTHING LIKE IT.**

I FIND THAT WRAPPING THE FISH IN FOIL MAKES IT EASIER TO HANDLE ON THE GRILL, AND IT NEVER STICKS. PLACING THE FOIL PACKAGES DIRECTLY ON THE DINNER PLATES ALLOWS YOUR GUESTS TO OPEN THEM AND ENJOY THE LOVELY AROMAS.

6 FILLETS (6 OUNCES EACH) SEA BASS OR 2 PIECES (2 POUNDS EACH)
WILD STRIPED BASS FILLETS

⅓ CUP LEMON JUICE

⅓ CUP EXTRA VIRGIN OLIVE OIL

3 LEMONS, SEEDED AND SLICED PAPER THIN

SEA SALT TO TASTE

1 BUNCH FRESH BASIL, LEAVES REMOVED, CUT IN CHIFFONADE (SEE NOTE)

Black sea bass and large wild striped bass are ideal for this recipe. But other fish can be used, including bluefish fillets, hake fillets, sablefish, and even halibut steaks. You could also prepare salmon this way, but if you like your salmon slightly underdone in the middle, reduce the cooking time somewhat. Puncturing holes in the top of the package for grilled fish allows for a little of the smoky flavor to penetrate. For small fillets in the oven, you can use cooking parchment instead of foil.

6 SERVINGS

Place the fish in a shallow dish and add the lemon juice and olive oil. Set aside at room temperature.

Preheat a grill or preheat the oven to 500 degrees.

For small fillets, arrange 6 pieces of foil large enough to enclose each fillet with room to spare, on a work surface. Place half the lemon slices in the middle of each, that is, about 3 slices of the lemon on each. Top the lemon slices with the fish, season the fish with sea salt, and cover with the remaining lemon slices.

Wrap each fillet loosely in the foil so there is air space inside, but seal the edges tightly. For larger fillets, use two sheets of heavy-duty foil and divide the ingredients between them. If you are grilling the fish, puncture about a dozen small holes in the top of the foil packages.

Place on the grill and grill the smaller fillets for about 15 minutes, or arrange on a baking sheet and place in the oven 10 minutes. Larger fillets will take 20 to 25 minutes on the grill or in the oven.

Open the top of each package and scatter with basil, then place the packages on a platter or on individual dinner plates and serve.

NOTE: The easiest way to shred basil is to stack 4 or 5 leaves, roll them up tightly, and slice them paper-thin, a preparation known as a chiffonade.

Baked Halibut Jardinière

My grandmother, who was a marvelous cook, was from Piraeus, Greece, the seaport just outside Athens. Originally her family came from Asia Minor, now Turkey, where the food is very similar to that of Greece. She would use local fish in Greece, but I substitute halibut, which is meaty, mild, and easy to find in my fish markets. Another option, in place of the halibut steaks, is to use thick fillets of halibut or some other fish, including red snapper.

4 halibut steaks, 1½ inches thick (about 2 pounds)

Salt and freshly ground black pepper

2 lemons

10 ounces fresh spinach, stemmed and well-rinsed

½ cup extra virgin olive oil

2 leeks, trimmed, well-washed, and sliced

1 medium onion, sliced thin

½ cup chopped celery

½ cup chopped fennel bulb

2 cups diced tomatoes, either fresh, peeled and seeded
(see sidebar, page 67), or canned

¼ cup chopped flat-leaf parsley

¼ cup chopped dill

4 SERVINGS

Season the fish on both sides with salt and pepper. Place on a plate and sprinkle with the juice of ½ lemon.

Place the spinach in a skillet over medium-high heat. Cook briefly, turning, just until the spinach wilts. Remove from heat and squeeze the spinach dry in several thicknesses of paper towel, or place the spinach in a potato ricer and press. Chop the spinach and set it aside. Wipe pan dry.

Heat half the oil in the skillet. Add the leeks, onion, celery, and fennel and cook over medium-low heat until soft but not brown. Add the tomatoes and spinach. Season the mixture with salt, pepper, and the juice of ½ lemon. Fold in parsley and dill.

Preheat the oven to 400 degrees.

Spread half the vegetable mixture in the bottom of a glass or ceramic baking dish. Place the fish on the vegetables and drizzle with 2 tablespoons of the remaining oil. Top with the remaining vegetables. Slice the remaining lemon thin, remove any seeds, and arrange the lemon slices decoratively on top.

Place in the oven and bake about 25 minutes, just until the point of a knife can easily separate the fish from the bone. Drizzle the remaining olive oil over the dish and serve.

Some rice, or simple boiled potatoes rolled in olive oil, salt, and
pepper are all that are needed alongside this dish.

ALICIA BOUZÁN-CORDON

Salt–Crusted Snapper from Barcelona

This is a typical fish preparation in Spain. My recipe comes from Barcelona. The crust of salt completely seals the fish so the result is more poached than baked but extremely succulent and juicy. I love to serve it with some homemade mayonnaise alongside as a sauce, some fresh steamed vegetables, and a bottle of albariño, a white wine from Galicia, in northwestern Spain. If you wish, you can add lemon halves and bunches of herbs to the cavity of the fish, for some added flavor.

I whole red snapper or sea bass (about 5 pounds),
cleaned, scaled, fins removed

Freshly ground black pepper

3 large egg whites

9 cups kosher salt

6 servings

Preheat the oven to 400 degrees.

Rinse the fish inside and out with cold water and pat dry with paper towels. Season the fish inside and out with pepper.

In a large bowl, mix the egg whites with ⅔ cup water and add the salt to make a paste. Spread half the salt paste over the bottom of an oval baking dish that is large enough to accommodate the fish, or on a large baking sheet lined with foil or in a disposable foil roasting pan. Place the fish on the salt paste and completely cover it with the rest of the salt paste.

Place it in the oven and bake for 40 to 45 minutes. The salt paste will have formed a hard crust.

To serve, bring the baking dish to the table or to a serving counter, or, if you did not use a baking dish, transfer the fish, in its crust, to a large platter. Gently crack the crust with a spoon. Lift off and discard the pieces of crust. Use a knife or a large spoon and a spatula to peel off the top skin and lift portions of the fish off the center bone.

When the top fillet has been served, discard the bone, and serve portions of the remaining fish, leaving the skin in the dish.

The technique for boning a whole cooked fish is not complicated and once mastered, makes for a showy bit of production at the table. Be sure to have an empty platter at hand for disposing of pieces of salt crust, fish skin, and bones. With salt-baked fish, once you have removed the top crust and lifted off the skin, you are ready to serve portions. Take a knife and cut along the entire back edge of the fish. Then cut two crosswise cuts down to the bone, to create three portions. Serve them. Then lift the bone out and discard it. Remove lemons and herbs if you used them. Cut the bottom fillet in thirds and lift them off the skin, and serve. And if there are connoisseurs at the table, be sure to offer them the fish's cheeks, the meaty nuggets just below the eyes. They are a delicacy.

Lemony Stuffed Sole Fillets

I STARTED COOKING THIS DISH FOR MY FAMILY YEARS AGO. IT'S EASY AND TASTY, AND I HAVE VARIED IT OVER TIME. THOUGH IT CAN BE MADE WITH BUTTER, THESE DAYS OLIVE OIL SEEMS MORE APPROPRIATE. THE ROLLED FILLETS CAN BE SERVED DIRECTLY FROM THE BAKING DISH, OR YOU COULD PLACE TWO ON EACH DINNER PLATE, WITH RICE OR POTATOES AND A VEGETABLE SIDE DISH.

4 MEDIUM TO LARGE FILLETS OF GRAY SOLE (1 1/2 TO 2 POUNDS)

SALT AND FRESHLY GROUND BLACK PEPPER

10 TABLESPOONS EXTRA VIRGIN OLIVE OIL

1 STALK CELERY, FINELY CHOPPED

1/2 MEDIUM ONION, FINELY CHOPPED

3/4 CUP PLAIN BREAD CRUMBS

1 TABLESPOON MINCED FLAT-LEAF PARSLEY LEAVES

1 TABLESPOON MINCED DILL

JUICE AND GRATED ZEST OF 1/2 LEMON

1/2 CUP DRY WHITE WINE

4 SERVINGS

Use a sharp knife to cut each fillet in half, lengthwise. There is a natural "seam" running down the middle of the fish to guide you. Season the pieces with salt and pepper and turn them so the whiter side is facing down.

Preheat the oven to 350 degrees. Use a little of the oil to grease a 9-inch square baking dish.

In a skillet, heat 3 tablespoons of the oil, add the celery and onion, and cook over medium-low heat until soft but not brown. Stir in the bread crumbs, parsley, half the dill, the lemon juice and zest.

Spoon about a tablespoon of this mixture in the middle of each piece of fish. Roll the fish pieces around the bread crumb mixture and place the rolls, seam side down, in the baking dish.

Mix the remaining olive oil with the wine and the remaining dill. Pour over the fish. Place in the oven and bake for 15 minutes. Baste the fish with the sauce in the pan, return it to the oven for another 5 minutes, and then serve.

This recipe can easily be dressed up a bit by tucking one or two peeled, deveined raw medium or small shrimp into the middle of each fish roulade. Just place the shrimp on top of the bread crumb stuffing before rolling up the strip of fillet.

Santa Barbara Seafood Stew

My friend in Santa Barbara, Mrs. Barnaby Conrad, got this recipe from a neighbor in 1972. I love its versatility. It can be a first course or a main course, for lunch or dinner. In Santa Barbara the weather is mild year-round, so I can always get the freshest fish. Elsewhere, I would serve it in summer. I dish it out of a big tureen and have plenty of crusty French bread on the side. Any leftovers can be pureed in a blender, stretched with more tomato, fish stock, or wine, if necessary, and served the next day as a French fish soup—*soupe de poissons*.

¼ cup extra virgin olive oil

½ cup finely chopped celery

½ cup finely chopped fennel bulb

1 cup chopped onion

4 cloves garlic, minced

⅓ cup Ricard or Pernod

1 cup dry white wine

4 cups clam juice or fish stock, or a mixture

3 cups tomato puree

1 teaspoon thyme leaves, preferably fresh

2 bay leaves

1 pound small white potatoes, halved

1 cup mayonnaise

Cayenne, to taste

Salt and freshly ground white pepper

6 servings

12 LARGE SHRIMP, PEELED

½ POUND SEA SCALLOPS, SIDE TENDON REMOVED

1 POUND SKINLESS HALIBUT, SEA BASS, OR HAKE FILLET, IN CHUNKS

SLICES OF BAGUETTE, TOASTED

Heat 2 tablespoons of the oil in a large pot or casserole, at least 4 quarts. Add the celery, fennel, onion, and 2 cloves of the garlic and sauté over low heat until the vegetables are soft but not brown. Stir in the Ricard or Pernod, wine, and clam juice. Bring to a simmer. Add the tomato puree, thyme, and bay leaves and simmer gently for about 20 minutes. Set aside until almost serving time.

Place the potatoes in a pot of salted water, bring to a simmer, and cook until just tender, about 15 minutes. Drain and set aside, covered.

Mix the mayonnaise with the remaining garlic, and, if desired, some cayenne, place this mixture in a small bowl for serving, and set aside.

About 15 minutes before serving time, bring the soup base to a simmer and season it to taste with salt and pepper and cayenne. Add the shrimp, allow them to cook about 5 minutes, then add the scallops. Cook them about 2 minutes, then add the fish. When the soup base returns to a simmer, turn off the heat. Reheat the potatoes.

If you wish to serve the fish stew from the cooking pot, bring it to the table with a ladle, or transfer it to a large bowl or tureen to serve it.

Serve the stew in flat soup plates, with a bowl of the potatoes alongside, and pass the garlic mayonnaise (aioli) and the toasted baguette slices along with it.

This stew is a close cousin to bouillabaisse. The principle is the same,
a tomato-based soup, enriched with wine, herbs, and vegetables.
Once that much is done, then the fish and seafood is added shortly
before serving, in stages, according to how long each will take to cook.

THE MAIN COURSE: POULTRY & MEAT

Melissa McGraw's Potato Chip Chicken

Muffie's Chicken with Mustard and Lemon

St. Barth's Chicken Brochettes

Chicken Scalloppini alla Pizzaiola

Chicken Cacciatore

Cider-Roasted Loin of Pork

Aunt Janet's Perfect Beef Tenderloin

Holiday Pot Roast

Sweet-and-Sour Meat Loaf

Goulash

Cardamom-Scented Lamb Stew

Left: Aunt Janet's Perfect Beef Tenderlion

Melissa McGraw's Potato Chip Chicken

*I*N LOOKING FOR A RECIPE USING THE SIMPLEST INGREDIENTS, YET ONE THAT COULD STILL BE SATISFYING AND MAGICAL, I BORROWED THIS FROM A DEAR FRIEND, MELISSA MCGRAW. SHE IN TURN, HAD INHERITED IT FROM HER MOTHER. AND LIKE ANYONE WHO ENJOYS COOKING FRESH, FAST, AND TASTY MEALS FOR FAMILY OR FRIENDS USING BASIC INGREDIENTS, I WAS QUICK TO ADOPT THIS RECIPE INTO MY HOUSEHOLD AS AN EASY WAY TO JAZZ UP A CASUAL SUPPER OR PICNIC. UNCOMPLICATED AND ACCESSIBLE, IT PROVIDES AN UNPRETENTIOUS MEAL AT THE SNAP OF A FINGER.

ONE FINAL NOTE: IT CAN BE ENJOYED HOT FROM THE OVEN OR AT ROOM TEMPERATURE. AND ANY LEFTOVERS CAN BE TURNED INTO A SPEEDY CHICKEN SALAD, SIMPLY DICED AND COMBINED WITH A GOOD-QUALITY COMMERCIAL MAYONNAISE.

6 TABLESPOONS UNSALTED BUTTER OR EXTRA VIRGIN OLIVE OIL

1 BAG (5 OUNCES) POTATO CHIPS

6 BONELESS, SKINLESS CHICKEN BREASTS (ABOUT 2 POUNDS)

1 LEMON

SALT AND FRESHLY GROUND BLACK PEPPER

Place the butter or oil in a baking dish large enough to hold the chicken in a single layer. Put the dish in the oven and turn the heat to 350 degrees. After a few minutes, when the butter has melted or the oil is hot, remove the dish from the oven. Let your oven continue to preheat.

Place the potato chips in a heavy plastic bag and crush them with a rolling pin to make fine crumbs.

Place the chicken in the baking dish and turn each breast to coat with butter or oil. Remove the chicken from the dish to a platter, then place the breasts, one at a time, in the plastic bag to coat with the potato chip crumbs. Place the coated chicken in the baking dish. Squeeze lemon over the chicken.

Cut the squeezed lemon in pieces and scatter these around the chicken in the dish. Season the chicken with salt and pepper. Bake 20 minutes. Serve hot or at room temperature.

NOTE: This recipe can be doubled or tripled for a buffet or party. For a buffet, depending on what else is served, you might want to try to find small chicken breasts, about 4 ounces each, or even cut regular ones in half. Divide them lengthwise for more attractive portions.

The author of this simple but effective recipe recommends using "light, baked" potato chips and a low-cholesterol butter substitute to cut fat and calories, but instead it was easier to reduce the amount of butter in the original recipe and use Yukon Gold potato chips. For a fine variation that is a tad less rich-tasting, you can substitute olive oil for the butter—no melting necessary—with olive oil potato chips. Using olive oil instead of butter is particularly appealing if the chicken is made in advance to be served cold.

Muffie's Chicken with Mustard and Lemon

THIS EASY, YUMMY, AND FAST RECIPE IS A "MUST" FOR ANYONE WITH NO EXTRA TIME ON THEIR HANDS. I CREATED THIS RECIPE ON THE SPUR OF THE MOMENT BECAUSE MY BOYFRIEND AT THE TIME WANTED TO EAT A HOME-COOKED MEAL FOR ONCE. HE DOUBTED THAT I COULD ACTUALLY COOK. I TOOK HIM UP ON THE CHALLENGE WITH THE REQUIREMENT THAT HE ASK NO QUESTIONS AND STAY OUT OF THE KITCHEN. I WENT TO THE SUPERMARKET AND GATHERED INGREDIENTS AND WINGED IT. BUT THE DISH WAS A SUCCESS, AND THE BOYFRIEND IS NOW MY HUSBAND.

½ CUP FLOUR

SALT AND FRESHLY GROUND BLACK PEPPER

2½ POUNDS BONELESS AND SKINLESS CHICKEN BREASTS
(EITHER 6 LARGE OR 8 SMALLER ONES)

5 TABLESPOONS EXTRA VIRGIN OLIVE OIL, APPROXIMATELY

¾ CUP DIJON-STYLE MUSTARD, OR TO TASTE

ZEST OF 1 LEMON

1½ CUPS DRY WHITE WINE

2 TABLESPOONS LEMON JUICE

Place the flour in a shallow soup plate and whisk in salt and pepper to taste. Dip each chicken breast in the seasoned flour to coat completely and set aside on a plate or a cutting board.

Place a skillet that will hold all the chicken breasts in a single layer over medium heat and add half the oil. Use two skillets if necessary, dividing the oil. Cook the chicken breasts in the oil, a few at a time, turning them once, and adding more oil as needed, until they are lightly browned on both sides. Remove them from the pan as they are lightly browned. They may not be completely cooked through.

Return all the chicken breasts to the pan or pans. Using half the mustard, coat one side of each chicken breast, season with salt and pepper, and then turn the chicken breasts over. Coat the second side of each piece of chicken with the mustard, scatter the lemon zest over them, and season with more salt and pepper if desired.

Pour in the wine and lemon juice, increase the heat to medium-high and cook the chicken about 5 minutes, basting it with the liquid in the pan until the breasts are cooked through. Remove the chicken breasts to a platter or a cutting board. Continue to cook the sauce in the pan, stirring it constantly, another couple of minutes, until it is the consistency of heavy cream. Taste for seasoning.

The chicken breasts can be served whole—best if you used the smaller ones—or, with the larger breasts, slice them on an angle about ½ inch thick, and arrange on a platter or on individual dinner plates. Briefly reheat the sauce and spoon it over the whole chicken breasts or slices, and serve.

Not only is this a lovely dinner-party dish and a good item for a buffet, it also works well on a picnic. The most important element, in preparing this dish, is to be sure that your chicken breasts are uniform in size, either small ones to serve whole or large ones to slice.

St. Barth's Chicken Brochettes

My mother-in-law told me she got this chicken recipe during a Caribbean vacation more than twenty years ago. A chef gave her the recipe after they had a conversation and discovered that they both spent time on Nantucket in the summer. With just one or two pieces of the chicken on short skewers, you have a nice party hors d'oeuvre. Use the marinade as a dipping sauce or serve the skewers with a commercial Asian peanut sauce.

2 POUNDS BONELESS AND SKINLESS CHICKEN BREASTS

2/3 CUP UNSWEETENED COCONUT MILK

1/3 CUP SOY SAUCE

1/3 CUP LIME JUICE

CAYENNE, TO TASTE

1/4 CUP CHICKEN STOCK

1 TABLESPOON DIJON-STYLE MUSTARD

1 1/2 TABLESPOONS FINELY MINCED SCALLIONS

You can use either regular coconut milk or the low-calorie "lite" kind for this recipe. If you keep canned coconut milk on your pantry shelf, store the cans upside down. That way you will not have all the thick part on the bottom. But turn the can right side up to open it.

6 SERVINGS

Cut the chicken breasts into nuggets about 1-inch square. You should have about 60.

In a bowl large enough to hold the chicken, mix the coconut milk, soy sauce, and lime juice. Season to taste with cayenne. Add the chicken pieces, turn to coat them and allow them to marinate 1 to 1½ hours.

Soak 12 wooden skewers, at least 8-inches long, in water.

Preheat a grill or a broiler.

Place 5 pieces of the chicken on each skewer. Grill or broil the chicken, about 3 minutes on each side, until lightly seared and cooked through. Remove the chicken to a serving platter and cover loosely with foil to keep warm.

Place the marinade in a saucepan and add the chicken stock and mustard. Simmer for about 10 minutes.

Serve two skewers per person, with some of the sauce poured over and scattered with the scallions.

Chicken Scalloppini alla Pizzaiola

This is my version of a dish that was inspired by one in Padma Lakshmi's cookbook *Easy Exotic* (Miramax Books, 2000). The main difference is that I use chicken, not veal. But I love the ease and versatility of this dish. You can always find the ingredients, you can make it in advance and reheat it, and even if you are stuck at the last minute, it doesn't take long to prepare.

⅓ cup flour

Salt and freshly ground black pepper

2 pounds boneless and skinless chicken breasts, in thin scalloppini cutlets

5 tablespoons extra virgin olive oil

2 teaspoons chopped fresh or dried rosemary leaves

1 teaspoon dried oregano

6 cloves garlic, peeled and smashed

20 plum tomatoes, cored and quartered, or 2 cans (28 ounces each)
plum tomatoes, well-drained and cut in halves or quarters

⅛ to ¼ teaspoon dried chili flakes, or to taste

4 tablespoons slivered fresh basil leaves

6 to 8 servings

Season the flour with salt and pepper. Cut the chicken so it is in uniform pieces, about 2 x 3 inches. Lightly dredge the chicken in the flour, shaking off the excess.

Heat 3 tablespoons of the oil in a large skillet over medium heat. Add the chicken and cook on both sides until lightly browned, removing the pieces to a platter as they are done.

Add the remaining oil to the skillet and add the rosemary, oregano, and garlic. Cook very briefly—do not allow the garlic to brown—and add the tomatoes and chili flakes. Cook about 5 minutes, stirring.

Return the chicken to the pan and simmer it briefly to reheat it. Taste the sauce and add more seasoning if needed. Transfer the chicken to a platter or to individual plates; scatter with basil and serve.

Many markets sell scalloppine-style chicken breasts, but if yours does not, it's easy enough to buy regular chicken breasts and just slice them through horizontally, with a sharp knife. Then put them between sheets of wax paper and pound them lightly. If you can find ripe plum tomatoes, by all means use them for a fresher flavor. But the dish is just fine with the canned kind.

Chicken Cacciatore

Don't you love a dish that becomes such a family favorite that family members request it and then clean their plates when it's served? This chicken cacciatore fits that description to a T! This is a recipe that suits an informal party, even one in the kitchen. The chicken is on the bone, which makes it succulent but not suitable for the most elegant dining. Some pasta, like fettuccine, would be delicious alongside to benefit from the sauce.

1 chicken (3½ pounds), cut into 8 pieces

Salt and freshly ground black pepper

½ teaspoon paprika

2 tablespoons extra virgin olive oil

1 medium onion, chopped

½ green bell pepper, seeded, cored, and cut into slivers

½ red bell pepper, seeded, cored, and cut into slivers

2 cloves garlic, minced

4 ounces cremini mushrooms, wiped clean, sliced

12 pitted olives, green or black, sliced

½ cup dry white wine

1 can (28 ounces) whole tomatoes, drained and crushed

1 teaspoon dried oregano

4 servings

Dry the chicken pieces on paper towels and season them with salt, pepper, and paprika.

Heat the oil in a large skillet and brown the chicken on all sides. Remove the pieces to a baking dish as they are browned.

Preheat the oven to 350 degrees.

Add the onion, green and red peppers, and garlic to the skillet and cook over medium heat until they are soft but not brown. Add the mushrooms and continue cooking until the mushrooms have wilted and are starting to brown. Stir in the olives, wine, tomatoes, and oregano. Season this mixture with salt and pepper.

Pour the sauce over the chicken and cook in the oven for about 45 minutes. The chicken is done when the juices run clear when the dark meat is poked with a small knife. Serve immediately.

A nice addition to this dish is some sweet or hot Italian sausage, or both, that you can brown after you have sautéed the chicken. Then slice the sausages and add them to the baking dish with the chicken. A pound of sausages, about 4 links, added to this dish will stretch it to serve 6. And the recipe can be doubled for buffet service.

Cider–Roasted Loin of Pork

THIS RECIPE FOR PORK LOIN WAS VOTED ONE OF THE BEST IN OUR FAMILY'S NEWSLETTER, "ROARING ROCK," WHERE I WRITE A COOKING COLUMN. MARINATING THE PORK OVERNIGHT IN CIDER AND SALT TENDERIZES THE MEAT, MAKES IT JUICY, AND BRINGS OUT ITS FLAVOR. THE PORK SLICES, GARNISHED WITH FRESH ROSEMARY, MAKE A VERY ATTRACTIVE PRESENTATION. THERE IS NO SAUCE COMPONENT, BUT SOME KIND OF CHUTNEY, A GOOD MUSTARD, OR EVEN HOMEMADE APPLESAUCE CAN BE SERVED ALONGSIDE.

1 QUART FRESH APPLE CIDER

¼ CUP KOSHER SALT OR SEA SALT

2 BONELESS PORK TENDERLOINS, ABOUT 1½ POUNDS EACH

2 TABLESPOONS EXTRA VIRGIN OLIVE OIL

1 TABLESPOON FRESHLY GROUND BLACK PEPPER

1 TABLESPOON CRUSHED DRIED ROSEMARY LEAVES

1 TABLESPOON GROUND SAGE

ROSEMARY SPRIGS FOR GARNISH

8 SERVINGS

Combine two cups of the cider, the salt, and 1 cup water in a saucepan and heat just until the salt dissolves. Allow to cool.

Place the pork loins in a heavy 1-gallon plastic bag with a zip closure. Add the cooled brine. Seal the bag and place on a dinner plate. Refrigerate overnight, 8 to 24 hours. Boil down the remaining 2 cups of cider until it has reduced to about ⅔ cup. Place in a container, cover, and refrigerate

Preheat the oven to 425 degrees. Remove the pork and the reduced cider from the refrigerator.

Remove the pork from the marinade and pat dry. Rub the loins with the oil, pepper, rosemary, and sage. Line a roasting pan with foil, place the pork on a rack in the roasting pan, and roast for 10 minutes. Baste the pork with the boiled cider, turning the loins to baste all around. Roast another 20 minutes, until an instant-read thermometer registers 150 degrees.

Remove the pork from the oven and let stand 10 minutes. Slice, arrange on a platter, garnish with rosemary, and serve.

In recent years, brining has become a popular way to enhance extremely lean meat, such as pork tenderloins, chicken, or turkey.

Aunt Janet's Perfect Beef Tenderloin

THIS RECIPE HAS BEEN IN THE FAMILY FOR YEARS, AND IT IS ALWAYS ON THE MENU FOR SPECIAL OCCASIONS AND HOLIDAYS. I LOVE IT BECAUSE IT COOKS ALL BY ITSELF, WITH NO TENDING.

1 CUP DRY RED WINE

1/4 CUP EXTRA VIRGIN OLIVE OIL

2 TABLESPOONS SOY SAUCE

2 TABLESPOONS WORCESTERSHIRE SAUCE

1 TEASPOON DRIED OREGANO

1 TEASPOON COARSELY GROUND BLACK PEPPER

1 CLOVE GARLIC, CHOPPED

1 BEEF TENDERLOIN (3 TO 4 POUNDS), TIED

2/3 CUP BEEF STOCK

2 TABLESPOONS TOMATO PASTE

1 TABLESPOON UNSALTED BUTTER

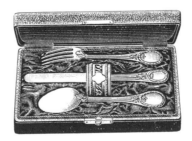

8 TO 12 SERVINGS

Combine the wine, olive oil, soy sauce, Worcestershire sauce, oregano, pepper, and garlic in a bowl. Place the beef tenderloin in a heavy 1-gallon plastic bag with a zip closure, pour in the wine mixture, seal, place on a platter or in a bowl, and refrigerate overnight.

Remove the marinating beef from the refrigerator for 1 hour before roasting. Preheat the oven to 500 degrees.

Place the tenderloin on a rack in a shallow roasting pan. Reserve the marinade.

Roast the tenderloin for 4 minutes per pound, for rare to medium-rare; 5 minutes per pound for medium. Immediately turn off the oven but leave the roast in the oven for 45 minutes without opening the oven door.

Remove the roast from the oven, transfer to a cutting board, and let stand at room temperature for 20 minutes before carving.

Strain the marinade into a saucepan. Add the stock and simmer for 10 minutes. Whisk in the tomato paste. Check seasoning. Gradually whisk in the butter, bit by bit. Remove the sauce from the heat.

Remove the trussing from the meat and slice it. Arrange it on a platter, gently reheat the sauce and serve it alongside.

NOTE: Another way to serve the beef, especially if you wish to prepare it in advance, is to slice it an inch thick after it has come out of the oven and cooled, and briefly sear the slices in a cast-iron pan. They will heat through and still be medium-rare in the middle.

The recipe is based on one that was developed for prime ribs of beef by Ann Seranne, a cookbook author who died in 1988. She had written a number of Junior League cookbooks. Her roast beef recipe, called "Always Rare," involved roasting the meat, which had to be at room temperature to start, for 5 minutes per pound at 500 degrees, then leaving it in the turned-off oven for 2 hours. The problem, with roast beef, was that the interior slices were always cool, but this version, for tenderloin, which is an unusual variation, is done in less time and does not suffer from the same problem.

EMILY SONNENBLICK, M.D. AND KEN OFFIT, M.D.

Holiday Pot Roast

This recipe is from my mother, who got it from other mothers at the Park School in Boston, Massachusetts, where I grew up. Ken and I like to make this fabulous pot roast for major holidays. When we make it, we do not blend the onions at the end of the recipe but leave them to drape over the meat. The pot roast is delicious served with potato pancakes, buttered mashed potatoes, egg noodles, or potato gnocchi, to help sop up the sauce.

¼ cup dark brown sugar

1 cup cider vinegar

2 cups tomato puree

1 tablespoon salt

¼ cup soy sauce

Freshly ground black pepper

1 teaspoon dried chili flakes, or to taste

2 bay leaves

1 rump roast (4 pounds)

4 medium onions, sliced thin

8 to 10 servings

Mix the brown sugar, vinegar, tomato puree, salt, soy sauce, pepper, and chili flakes in a bowl. Add the bay leaves.

Place the meat in a heavy 1-gallon plastic bag with a zip closure. Pour the marinade mixture into the bag and seal it. Place the bag in a bowl and refrigerate overnight and up to 36 hours, turning it from time to time.

Allow the meat to come to room temperature. Preheat the oven to 300 degrees.

Place the meat and the marinade in an ovenproof casserole. Scatter the onions on top. Bake uncovered for 4 hours, until it is tender, turning the meat in the sauce every half hour.

Remove the meat from the sauce and place on a cutting board. Puree the sauce, either with the onions, which will make it thicker, or without, in a blender and transfer it to a saucepan to reheat. Check the seasoning.

To serve, slice the meat and arrange it on a platter, with some of the sauce spooned over it and the rest passed alongside. Alternatively, the sliced meat can be gently reheated in the sauce.

The vinegar in the marinade makes this pot roast similar to sauerbraten. You can also reduce the vinegar to ½ cup and substitute beef stock for the rest. Though a rump roast is a reliable cut for potting, there are other cuts, including brisket and chuck roasts that can be used. And like most stewed meats, this one is better made in advance and reheated. It becomes much easier to slice after it has cooled from the initial baking.

Sweet-and-Sour Meat Loaf

*T*HE MOTHER OF MY FRIEND BARBARA CURRY ORIGINATED THIS RECIPE. IT'S GREAT FOR A FAMILY DINNER WITH MASHED POTATOES AND GREEN BEANS. AND FOR A DINNER PARTY? IT'S COMFORT FOOD AND SUITABLE FOR A CASUAL GATHERING, ON A SUNDAY NIGHT, FOR EXAMPLE. THE MEN WILL LOVE IT! AND LEFTOVER SLICES ARE FABULOUS FOR SANDWICHES THE NEXT DAY, FOR LUNCH OR FOR A PICNIC.

1 CUP CRUSHED CANNED TOMATOES

4 TABLESPOONS LIGHT BROWN SUGAR

2 TABLESPOONS RED WINE VINEGAR

2 TEASPOONS DIJON-STYLE MUSTARD

2 POUNDS GROUND BEEF

1 CUP DRY BREAD CRUMBS

1 TEASPOON SALT, OR TO TASTE

1/4 TEASPOON FRESHLY GROUND BLACK PEPPER

2 TABLESPOONS GRATED ONION

1 LARGE EGG

There are many options when it comes to ground beef. The leanest kind, with only 10 percent fat, may result in meat loaf that is on the dry side. A better choice is beef that is 75 to 80 percent lean, and sirloin or chuck will have better flavor than round.

6 SERVINGS

Simmer the tomatoes, sugar, vinegar, and mustard together just until the sugar dissolves. Remove from the heat.

Preheat the oven to 350 degrees.

Mix the beef with the bread crumbs, salt, pepper, onion, and egg. Add ¾ cup of the tomato mixture. Form into a loaf, place in a baking dish, and cover with foil. Bake for 30 minutes.

Remove the foil from the meat loaf and spread the remaining tomato mixture over the loaf. Bake for 30 minutes longer. Serve hot or cold.

Goulash

*M*Y SON FOUND THIS RECIPE AND MADE THE GOULASH FOR ME, AND I HAVE KEPT IT BECAUSE I LIKED IT BETTER THAN MY OWN. IT'S EXTREMELY EASY TO MAKE IN ADVANCE AND EVEN TO FREEZE AND REHEAT FOR A PARTY. IT ALLOWS ME TO SPEND TIME WITH MY GUESTS INSTEAD OF IN THE KITCHEN.

2 TABLESPOONS EXTRA VIRGIN OLIVE OIL

1 CUP CHOPPED ONION

3 CLOVES GARLIC, MINCED

3 TABLESPOONS SWEET HUNGARIAN PAPRIKA

1 TEASPOON DRIED MARJORAM

1 TABLESPOON WHITE WINE VINEGAR

JUICE AND GRATED ZEST OF 1/2 LEMON

SALT AND FRESHLY GROUND BLACK PEPPER

3 TABLESPOONS TOMATO PASTE

2 TO 3 CUPS BEEF STOCK

3 1/2 POUNDS VEAL SHOULDER IN 2-INCH CUBES FOR STEW

1 TABLESPOON MINCED FRESH MARJORAM LEAVES

1 1/2 CUPS SOUR CREAM FOR SERVING

8 SERVINGS

Heat the oil in a heavy 5-quart casserole. Add the onion and cook over medium-low heat, stirring, until it is golden brown, about 10 minutes. Add the garlic, stir briefly, then stir in the paprika and marjoram. Cook for about 30 seconds, then stir in the vinegar, lemon juice and zest, and salt and pepper to taste. Cook for another 2 minutes.

Add the tomato paste and stir well; allow it to cook for about 3 minutes. Add the stock and stir to dissolve the tomato paste. Bring the mixture to a simmer.

Add the meat. Simmer, uncovered, for about 1½ hours, until the meat is tender. Stir from time to time and add more stock if needed. The goulash should have plenty of sauce but not be soupy. To serve, dust with marjoram. Serve with sour cream on the side.

NOTE: Though the goulash can be made with beef stew meat, it's somewhat lighter and will cook faster with veal. Try to find real Hungarian paprika for this recipe. It has much more flavor than the ordinary supermarket kind.

The obvious accompaniment for goulash would be a bowl of buttered broad egg noodles or, if you can find it, spaetzle. Dust the noodles or spaetzle with poppy seeds for a real Hungarian touch. With this dish, any leftovers can be turned into what the Hungarians call goulash soup. Simply dice the leftover meat into small pieces and thin the sauce with stock or water, heat it, adjust the seasoning, and you have soup. Serve it with little boiled potatoes and sour cream.

Cardamom–Scented Lamb Stew

I FIRST TASTED THIS STEW ABOUT TWENTY-FIVE YEARS AGO. IT HAD BEEN PREPARED BY MY FATHER'S COOK, A FORMER AIRLINE PILOT FROM GERMANY. SHE LOVED TO USE EXOTIC SPICES. THIS RECIPE, WHICH I PUBLISHED IN MY FAMILY'S NEWSLETTER, RESULTS IN A RICH BUT SUBTLY FLAVORED STEW THAT MAKES A TERRIFIC HEARTY SUPPER ON COLD DAYS WITH JUST A HINT OF SPRING IN THE AIR. THE FLAVOR IS ACTUALLY RICHER IF THE STEW IS MADE A FEW HOURS OR A DAY IN ADVANCE AND REHEATED. I RECOMMEND SERVING IT WITH COUSCOUS AND ASPARAGUS. I HAVE ALSO MADE THIS STEW USING VEAL INSTEAD OF LAMB. AS VEAL IS LESS FATTY THAN LAMB, DREDGE THE VEAL CUBES IN FLOUR BEFORE BROWNING TO SEAL IN MOISTURE, AND ADD ADDITIONAL BUTTER OR OIL BEFORE SAUTÉING THE VEGETABLES.

THERE IS A WHIFF OF INDIA IN THIS RECIPE, SO BASMATI RICE WOULD ALSO BE PERFECT ALONGSIDE IT.

3 CLOVES GARLIC

3 STALKS CELERY

2 CARROTS, PEELED

1 MEDIUM ONION

A ROUND OF FRESH GINGER ABOUT ½ INCH THICK, PEELED

4 TABLESPOONS EXTRA VIRGIN OLIVE OIL

4 POUNDS WELL-TRIMMED LAMB SHOULDER OR LEG, CUT INTO 1-INCH CUBES

3 TABLESPOONS GROUND CARDAMOM

2 CUPS CHICKEN STOCK

12 SMALL RED POTATOES, WASHED BUT NOT PEELED

Salt and freshly ground black pepper

1 cup unsweetened coconut milk

Juice and grated zest of 1 lime

3 tablespoons finely chopped fresh mint leaves

1/2 cup finely chopped cilantro leaves

Using a grating blade of a food processor, grate the garlic, celery, carrots, onion, and ginger. Set aside.

Heat the olive oil in a 5- to 7-quart casserole. Dry the lamb and add as much of it to the casserole as will fit without crowding; brown the cubes over medium-high heat. Remove the lamb to a platter and keep adding more until all are browned.

Reduce the heat to low. Add the grated vegetables and cook, stirring frequently, until tender and starting to brown, about 10 minutes. Add the cardamom, cook for another 2 minutes, then stir in the stock.

Return the lamb, including any collected juices, to the casserole and add the potatoes. Season with salt and pepper to taste. Simmer, covered, over low heat for about 1 hour. The lamb will be not quite tender.

Stir in the coconut milk. Continue to simmer the stew for 30 minutes or until the lamb is tender. Stir in the lime juice and check seasoning.

Mix the lime zest, mint, and cilantro together and place in a small dish. Serve the stew in its casserole or in a shallow bowl, with the zest and herb garnish alongside for sprinkling on each portion.

*Lamb shoulder is neither as lean nor as tender as the leg.
But it is more succulent, and with slow cooking, as in this recipe,
it will become moist and tender. The risk with the leg is that the
meat may be dry, even when stewed.*

STUNNING SIDES

Iceberg Wedges with Blue Cheese Dressing

Colorful Chinese Coleslaw

Perfect Potato Salad

Fine-Tuned Green Beans with Feta

Summer Corn Salad

Warm Corn and Prosciutto

Puree of Peas and Watercress

Mushrooms with Pine Nuts

Asian Asparagus Stir-Fry

Herbed Orzo with Toasted Pine Nuts

Nutted Wild Rice

Seasoned Party Rice

Timbales of Smashed Garlic Potatoes

Swiss Chard and Potatoes

Gramma Betty's Favorite Stuffed Potatoes

Left: Fine-Tuned Green Beans with Feta

Iceberg Wedges with Blue Cheese Dressing

My old, reliable blue cheese dressing is so adaptable! I got the recipe from a family friend years ago, who in turn got it from a friend in California. It's been around for decades! I like it best over wedges of crisp iceberg lettuce, sometimes with crumbled bacon scattered on top. It makes a wonderful dip for crudités or a dressing for cold seafood such as lump crabmeat. To use this dressing as a dip, it is best to make it quite smooth: force the cheese through a sieve before mixing it with the other ingredients.

1 cup mayonnaise

3/4 cup buttermilk or plain yogurt

2 teaspoons Worcestershire sauce

1 small clove garlic, forced through a press

Freshly ground black pepper

4 ounces crumbled blue cheese

1 head iceberg lettuce, outer leaves removed, core trimmed

1/2 pound country bacon, cooked and crumbled,
or 8 slices prosciutto, optional

8 servings

Thin the mayonnaise with the buttermilk or yogurt. Stir in the Worcestershire sauce and garlic, and season with pepper to taste. Fold in the blue cheese.

Cut the lettuce into 8 wedges and place on salad plates. Spoon the dressing over each wedge and, if desired, scatter with crumbled bacon or drape a slice of prosciutto on top of each. Serve.

Though many kinds of somewhat dry-textured blue cheeses are easy to crumble, especially Roquefort and American Maytag blue, there are containers of crumbled blue cheese sold in supermarkets and cheese shops, which represent a worthwhile shortcut.

Colorful Chinese Coleslaw

THIS RECIPE WAS PASSED ON TO ME BY A FRIEND, WHO PREPARED IT FOR A LARGE BUFFET. EVERYONE WAS WILD ABOUT IT THAT DAY. THEN WHEN I MADE IT FOR A FAMILY REUNION, IT GOT THE SAME RESPONSE. IT IS DELICIOUS AND HAS AN UNUSUAL FLAVOR, AND IS A REAL DEPARTURE FROM YOUR STANDARD COLESLAW. IF YOU OWN ANY CHINESE OR ASIAN SERVING DISHES OR IMPLEMENTS, THIS IS THE SALAD THAT DESERVES THEIR USE. A PLAIN PORCELAIN BOWL PLACED INTO A BAMBOO BASKET OR EVEN INTO THE BASE OF A BIG BAMBOO STEAMER WOULD BE A STYLISH ALTERNATIVE.

½ LARGE HEAD CHINESE NAPA CABBAGE

8 SCALLIONS, TRIMMED, SOME GREEN LEFT ON, CHOPPED

3 LARGE CARROTS, PEELED AND IN JULIENNE

¼ CUP SESAME SEEDS

2½ OUNCES THIN DRIED CURLY JAPANESE NOODLES (SUCH AS RAMEN)

½ CUP RICE VINEGAR

½ CUP GRAPESEED, CANOLA, OR PEANUT OIL

1 TABLESPOON SOY SAUCE

1 TABLESPOON ASIAN TOASTED SESAME OIL

2 TEASPOONS SUGAR

FRESHLY GROUND BLACK PEPPER

½ CUP CHOPPED CILANTRO LEAVES

Cut out the core of the cabbage and slice it crosswise, very thin. Place it in a very large bowl with the scallions and carrots.

Place the sesame seeds in a skillet over medium heat and toast until very lightly browned. Add to the bowl.

Place the noodles in a plastic bag and crush with a rolling pin. Add to the bowl.

Combine the rice vinegar, oil, soy sauce, sesame oil, and sugar in a separate bowl. Beat to combine, then pour over the vegetables in the large bowl. Season to taste with pepper. Cover and refrigerate at least 3 hours or overnight.

To serve, toss ingredients and fold in cilantro.

*Though you can make this slaw using regular red or white cabbage,
it has a unique crispness and a distinctive flavor when you use
Chinese napa cabbage, the kind that comes in big, oblong heads.
The dried noodles soften in the dressing but contribute to the texture
of the salad, and the addition of soy sauce and Asian toasted sesame
oil adds to its flavor profile. Wait until serving time to fold in the
cilantro, so it does not get soggy.*

Perfect Potato Salad

This is my "never-fail" salad. I bring it to every potluck from family functions to church parties. It's always a big hit and incredibly easy. The salad is delicious when mixed while the potatoes are still a little warm, and served immediately without refrigerating it. But if you do make it in advance and place it in the refrigerator, be sure to allow it to come to room temperature for about an hour before serving.

3 pounds Red Bliss potatoes (about 24), quartered

Salt, to taste

2 cups finely chopped red onion

2 tablespoons white wine vinegar

1 tablespoon sugar

2 tablespoons celery seeds

3 cups mayonnaise

Freshly ground black pepper, to taste

2 tablespoons finely minced chives

Place the potatoes in a 3-quart saucepan, cover with salted water, bring to a boil, reduce heat, and simmer until just tender, about 15 minutes.

Transfer to a large mixing bowl, add the onion, sprinkle with the vinegar, and gently mix.

Mix the sugar, celery seeds, and mayonnaise together in a small bowl. Season with salt and pepper. Fold into the potato mixture. Cover and refrigerate until ready to serve.

Just before serving, add the chives. Check seasoning and add more salt and pepper if needed.

8 SERVINGS

There are thousands of ways to make potato salad. This one is quite foolproof. You can vary it to taste, for example, by using chopped scallions in place of the red onion, eliminating the celery seeds, or even bolstering the celery flavor by adding chopped celery and finely minced celery leaves. A dollop of mustard in the dressing, or a dressing made of half mayonnaise and half yogurt are some other possibilities.

Fine-Tuned Green Beans with Feta

My cousin Liz Tallery lives in Virginia. She and I got married within a month of each other, and she insisted that any self-respecting girl from Virginia should have a repertoire of easy dishes that could be made on a moment's notice and were sure to please. If we could achieve this, everyone would assume we could cook anything.

When we visited the Tallerys at their farm in northern Virginia, Saturday mornings involved long hikes in the Blue Ridge Mountains and the afternoons were devoted to fine-tuning these "easy" recipes. Most of them were designed to be served with our "never-fail" recipe for beef tenderloin. They were also designed so we didn't have to be off in the kitchen once the fun got started. We wanted to be in the living room where the action was, having cocktails with everyone. That's why we serve the beans at room temperature.

Salt

1 pound fresh green beans, ends trimmed

1 tablespoon red wine vinegar

3 tablespoons extra virgin olive oil

1 teaspoon Dijon mustard

1/2 pound feta cheese, preferably Greek, drained and crumbled

Freshly ground black pepper

6 SERVINGS

Have a large bowl of ice cubes ready. Bring a 3-quart pot of well-salted water to a boil. Add the beans and blanch them about 6 minutes, until they are tender. Drain and place the beans in the bowl of ice cubes, turning them several times, to chill them down.

In a large bowl, beat the vinegar, oil, and mustard together. Fold in the feta. Drain the cooled beans, spread them on paper towels to pat dry and then add them, tossing them with the dressing. Set them aside at room temperature until it's time to serve them.

NOTE: You can substitute blue cheese or ricotta salata for the feta.

These beans will be tender, but if you prefer them to be crisper, you can shave a few minutes off the cooking time. It's a matter of taste. The extra step of placing the beans—or other blanched vegetables—in ice is what chefs do to stop the cooking and set the color. It's something to remember when you are cooking other green vegetables like broccoli and asparagus. The recipe, doubled, makes a superb addition to a buffet table either indoors, or, in summer, outdoors for a party on a terrace or by the pool, when the tenderloin to go with it can sizzle on the grill. Pile the beans and their dressing into a container, and you have a dish for a picnic or a cookout at the beach.

Summer Corn Salad

*I*FIRST HAD THIS SALAD IN THE SUMMER AT A FAMILY LUNCHEON IN A BEAUTIFUL
GARDEN ON THE NORTH SHORE OF LONG ISLAND. IT WAS AT A CHILDREN'S
BIRTHDAY PARTY. THE CHILDREN WERE EATING PIZZA, BUT THE HOSTESS
PREPARED A LOVELY COLD BUFFET FOR THE ADULTS AND THIS SALAD WAS ONE OF THE DISHES.
IT'S SO EASY TO MAKE IN THE SUMMER WHEN FRESH CORN AND TOMATOES BECKON FROM
FARM STANDS. THE AVOCADO AND CILANTRO GIVE IT AN ALMOST MEXICAN ZING. I LOVE IT
WITH BARBECUED CHICKEN, A PLATTER OF TOMATOES AND MOZZARELLA, AND SOME YUMMY
DESSERTS. THE CORN REALLY BRIGHTENS THE BUFFET TABLE. FOR ADDED EYE-APPEAL,
CONSIDER SERVING THE SALAD IN SCOOPED-OUT TOMATO HALVES.

10 TO 12 SERVINGS

8 EARS OF YELLOW CORN, SHUCKED

2 CUPS DICED CHERRY TOMATOES

4 AVOCADOES, PITTED, PEELED, AND DICED

JUICE OF 3 LIMES

1/2 CUP EXTRA VIRGIN OLIVE OIL

SALT AND PEPPER TO TASTE

1/2 CUP FINELY CHOPPED CILANTRO LEAVES (ABOUT 1 BUNCH)

Bring a large pot of water to a boil, add the corn, and when the water returns to the boil, turn off heat. Cover and let stand 10 minutes. Remove the corn from the pot and allow to cool. Cut the kernels from the cobs and place in a large bowl.

Fold in the tomatoes and avocadoes.

Beat the lime juice and olive oil together and season to taste with salt and pepper. Fold the dressing into the corn mixture. Fold in the cilantro.

The salad is ready to serve.

The method for cooking corn-on-the-cob, by bringing a pot of water to a boil, putting the corn in, and shutting off the water as soon as it returns to the boil is foolproof. And you do not need any sugar or salt in the water because the corn is not in there long enough for any seasoning to matter. The best way to strip the kernels from the cobs is to hold the ear of corn vertically in a large, shallow bowl and cut off the kernels with a sharp knife. With the corn in the bowl, the kernels are less likely to fly all over the kitchen. There are special gadgets sold for stripping the kernels, but they are not really necessary.

It's time-consuming to pluck the leaves from the stems of cilantro, but the end result is much more appealing than having bits of stem mixed in with the herb.

Warm Corn and Prosciutto

I LOVE THIS IN THE SUMMER FOR LUNCH OR AS A STARTER WHEN FRIENDS COME FOR DINNER. KIDS ALSO LOVE THIS DISH. I FIRST HAD IT YEARS AND YEARS AGO, AT A LUNCH AT LEE BAILEY'S HOUSE. HE WAS A GREAT SOUTHERN COOK AND AUTHOR; HE GAVE ME THE RECIPE AND HE EVEN INCLUDED IT IN ONE OF HIS BOOKS. IT IS ONE OF MY FAVORITE EAST HAMPTON DISHES, AND I LOVE IT WITH LOBSTER IN THE SUMMER, BUT IT'S ALSO DELICIOUS WITH SAUTÉED SHRIMP. SERVE A BIG PLATTER OF SLICED TOMATOES WITH IT, AND WEDGES OF CANTALOUPE AFTER THE MAIN COURSE, AND YOU KNOW IT'S SUMMER.

6 SERVINGS

*Though this dish is excellent as a side dish, to be spooned out from a big
bowl, it can also be used as a bed on which to put fillets of grilled fish.*

1 TABLESPOON UNSALTED BUTTER

10 EARS CORN, PREFERABLY WHITE, KERNELS STRIPPED FROM COB

2 TABLESPOONS HALF-AND-HALF

SALT AND FRESHLY GROUND BLACK PEPPER

6 OUNCES PROSCIUTTO, CUT INTO THIN STRIPS

Heat the butter in a large sauté pan over medium heat. When it starts to bubble,
add the corn. Reduce the heat, add the half-and-half, and cook over low heat until
the corn is just tender, 5 minutes. Season with salt and pepper to taste.

Remove from the heat and fold in the prosciutto. Allow to cool 15 minutes
before transferring to a serving dish.

NOTE: When you buy prosciutto for this dish, ask for slices that are not too thin,
about ⅛ inch thick is best. That way it's easier to cut very thin strips of the ham.

BARBARA GIMBEL

Puree of Peas and Watercress

THIS RECIPE DOES NOT COME WITH ANY STORY. IT'S JUST A SIMPLE, CONVENIENT DINNER-PARTY VEGETABLE THAT IS COLORFUL AND EXCELLENT TO SERVE WITH ROAST RACK OF LAMB. IT IS ALSO GOOD ALONGSIDE GRILLED FISH AND MAKES A BEAUTIFUL BED FOR SALMON FILLETS SAUTÉED IN BUTTER.

2 POUNDS FROZEN BABY PEAS

4 BUNCHES WATERCRESS, TRIMMED OF ALL BUT THE TOP 3 INCHES

6 TABLESPOONS UNSALTED BUTTER, DICED

SALT AND FRESHLY GROUND BLACK PEPPER

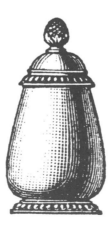

8 SERVINGS

Fill a large saucepan with water and bring it to a boil. Add the peas and when the water returns to a boil, add the watercress tops, remove from the heat, and cover the saucepan.

Allow it to sit for 5 minutes so the watercress wilts. Pour the contents of the pot into a colander and drain well.

Transfer the peas and watercress to a food processor, in batches if they do not all fit at once. Add some or all of the butter, depending on how much of the peas and watercress are in the food processor. Blend until smooth. Season to taste with salt and pepper.

Return the puree to the saucepan and gently reheat before serving.

Frozen baby peas are somewhat unique. It is almost impossible to buy fresh baby peas, even when farm stands sell peas in June. They have garden peas or English peas but not baby peas, which are much sweeter. The closest substitute for the frozen peas would be to shell sugar snap peas, a foolish thing to do because it means wasting the crunchy sweet pods. So frozen peas it is.

The puree has a little texture. If you want it to be perfectly smooth, either process it in a blender or force it through a sieve or a food mill after it comes out of the food processor.

Mushrooms with Pine Nuts

I MADE THIS RECIPE UP—IT'S SOMETHING I OFTEN DO—USING THE INGREDIENTS I LOVE. I DEVELOPED A PASSION FOR PINE NUTS ON A TRIP TO ITALY. THE MUSHROOMS ARE DELICIOUS WITH MEAT OR FISH OR EVEN MIXED INTO FRESH SPINACH.

1 CUP PINE NUTS

2 TABLESPOONS EXTRA VIRGIN OLIVE OIL

1 POUND CREMINI MUSHROOMS, WIPED CLEAN AND SLICED

1/3 CUP DRY WHITE WINE OR DRY SHERRY

SALT AND FRESHLY GROUND BLACK PEPPER

2 TABLESPOONS UNSALTED BUTTER

Heat a large sauté pan. Add the pine nuts and cook over medium heat until they are toasted. Set them aside.

Heat the oil in the pan. Add the mushrooms and cook over medium heat until they are just wilted. Pour the wine into the pan and cook a few minutes, until the liquid moistens the mushrooms without being soupy. Season the mushrooms with salt and pepper and add the nuts.

Stir in the butter about ½ tablespoon at a time, to enrich and thicken the sauce. Serve at once.

NOTE: If you prepare this dish up to the point of adding the butter, it can be set aside until serving time. Then reheat the mushrooms, add in the butter, and serve.

4 TO 6 SERVINGS

You do not need fancy mushrooms to make this dish. Cremini mushrooms, the kind that are shaped like regular white mushrooms but are a beige color, are fine. They do have more flavor than plain white mushrooms. Shiitakes, with their stems removed, will also work extremely well in this recipe.

Asian Asparagus Stir-Fry

I TOOK A PRIVATE CHINESE COOKING CLASS YEARS AGO. EVEN WHEN THE MEAL IS NOT CHINESE, I FIND THIS DISH TO BE POPULAR AND EASY TO PREPARE IN QUANTITY. UNLESS YOU PLAN TO DISH THE ASPARAGUS OUT ONTO INDIVIDUAL PLATES IN THE KITCHEN, A CHINESE PORCELAIN BOWL WOULD BE THE PERFECT CONTAINER FOR THIS RECIPE.

8 LARGE DRIED CHINESE BLACK MUSHROOMS

2 POUNDS ASPARAGUS

3 TABLESPOONS PEANUT OR CANOLA OIL

1½ CUPS SLICED CANNED BAMBOO SHOOTS, DRAINED AND SLIVERED

1 TEASPOON SUGAR

2 TABLESPOONS SOY SAUCE

SALT TO TASTE

Place the mushrooms in a dish, add warm water to cover, and set aside to soak for 30 minutes.

Meanwhile, snap the ends off the asparagus, rinse them, and slice the spears on the diagonal into 1-inch pieces.

When the mushrooms have softened, remove them from the liquid. Strain and reserve ¼ cup of the liquid. Pat the mushrooms dry on paper towels and slice them.

Heat the oil in a wok or a large skillet and add the mushrooms. Stir-fry for a minute. Add the bamboo shoots and mix. Add the asparagus and mix well. Add the sugar, soy sauce, about a teaspoon of salt, and the reserved mushroom liquid. Cover the pan and cook for about 5 minutes.

Taste for seasoning and add more salt if needed. Serve at once.

6 TO 8 SERVINGS

One aspect of this dish that makes it especially convenient is that when
the asparagus are slant-cut in small pieces, they do not have to be
peeled as they would if you served whole spears. The recipe can be
prepared in advance up to the point of adding the asparagus. But that
part only takes a few minutes and then your dish is ready to serve.

JANE BOWLING

Herbed Orzo with Toasted Pine Nuts

A FRIEND WHO HAD A BEAUTIFUL SUMMER HOME IN THE BERKSHIRES GAVE ME THIS RECIPE. WE WOULD HAVE DINNER AT HER LONG RUSTIC WOOD TABLE SET ON HER LARGE SCREENED PORCH, WITH BUNCHES OF FRESH FLOWERS EVERYWHERE. IT WAS ALWAYS MAGICAL, AND WHENEVER I SERVE THIS DISH IT REMINDS ME OF PERFECT SUMMER EVENINGS WITH FRIENDS, AWAY FROM THE HECTIC ROUTINE OF THE CITY. I LOVE TO SERVE IT ALONGSIDE GRILLED MEAT OR FISH. AS AN ALTERNATIVE PRESENTATION FOR THIS SIDE DISH, CONSIDER PILING IT IN THE CENTER OF A PLATTER AND PLACING GRILLED CHICKEN BREASTS, PORK CHOPS, OR JUMBO SHRIMP AROUND THE ORZO.

6 SERVINGS

SALT

2 CUPS ORZO

⅓ CUP PINE NUTS

4 TABLESPOONS EXTRA VIRGIN OLIVE OIL

JUICE OF 1 LEMON

FRESHLY GROUND BLACK PEPPER

½ CUP FINELY CHOPPED CILANTRO LEAVES

½ CUP FINELY CHOPPED MINT LEAVES

Bring 6 cups of salted water to a boil and add the orzo. Cook until al dente, about 8 minutes.

While the orzo is cooking, place the pine nuts in a skillet over medium heat and cook, stirring frequently, until the nuts are uniformly toasted. Transfer them to a large bowl.

When the orzo is done, drain it well and transfer it to the bowl. Add the olive oil, lemon juice, and salt and pepper to taste. Allow the mixture to cool to room temperature, then fold in the cilantro and mint and toss. Serve at room temperature.

Other small pasta can be used in place of the orzo. Israeli couscous, which is large and rounded, makes an excellent alternative. And other ingredients, such as diced fresh tomatoes or peppers, finely chopped sautéed mushrooms, or zucchini can also be folded in.

ANNETTE RICKEL

Nutted Wild Rice

My grandmother had a farm in northern Michigan, in the heart of the duck-hunting region, and she came up with this recipe to serve with wild duck. What makes it special for me is that it brings back memories of country gatherings at my grandparents' farm for a wonderful dinner after my father and grandfather returned from hunting. It's a dish I like to make in fall or winter. It would be perfect at Thanksgiving, and, fully cooked, it can also be used to stuff Cornish hens or baby chickens. I like to serve it in a glass-lined silver bowl. It's very portable—perfect for potluck suppers—because it is not meant to be served piping hot.

1 package (6 ounces) wild rice

5 cups chicken stock

1 cup pecan halves

1 cup golden raisins

Grated zest of 1 orange

1/3 cup finely chopped mint leaves

1/3 cup thinly sliced scallions

1/3 cup freshly squeezed orange juice

1/4 cup extra virgin olive oil

Salt and freshly ground black pepper, to taste

Place the rice in a sieve and rinse it under cold running water. Transfer it to a medium-size saucepan, add the stock, bring to a boil, and lower the heat to a gentle simmer. Cook for about 45 minutes, until the rice is tender.

Line a colander with a thin kitchen towel or several thicknesses of paper towel, pour in the rice and allow it to drain. Transfer the rice to a bowl.

Fold in the remaining ingredients and toss gently. Allow the mixture to stand at room temperature for 2 hours, check seasonings, and serve.

Wild rice is actually a type of grass, not a rice at all. And there are two kinds: The extra-fancy, smooth, almost black kind comes from California and Minnesota but it is not truly wild, despite drawings of Indians in canoes that may appear on the package. It is a cultivated version of wild rice, often called paddy rice, and is harvested by machine. Traditional wild rice that is harvested by Indians in the northern Great Lakes is much harder to find. It is sold online, available from sites such as www.nativeharvest.com. The grains may be broken, and they are somewhat lighter in color and not as handsome because they have been threshed by hand. This traditional kind of wild rice is also more expensive, but it cooks faster, fluffs up better, and yields about 20 percent more grain after cooking. The flavor of true wild rice is similar to that of paddy rice, but it has a noticeably more tender bite.

Seasoned Party Rice

SOME KIND OF GRAIN DISH IS USUALLY A MUST TO ROUND OUT A MAIN COURSE AT A DINNER. THIS ONE, WITH ITS RATHER DELICATE TOUCH OF ASIAN SEASONING, COULD ACCOMPANY MEAT, FISH, OR POULTRY. THE USE OF JASMINE RICE GIVES THE DISH A LOVELY FRAGRANCE, BUT IF YOU CAN'T FIND IT, BASMATI RICE WOULD BE A GOOD ALTERNATIVE. WHEN SERVING, INSTEAD OF SIMPLY PILING RICE IN A BOWL OR SPOONING IT OUT ONTO DINNER PLATES, PACK THE RICE INTO LIGHTLY OILED MUFFIN CUPS OR RAMEKINS AND UNMOLD TIMBALE-SHAPED MOUNDS ONTO EACH PLATE.

2 TABLESPOONS EXTRA VIRGIN OLIVE OIL

1 MEDIUM ONION, FINELY CHOPPED

1 1/2 TEASPOONS FINELY MINCED FRESH GINGER

1 1/2 TEASPOONS DRY MUSTARD

1 1/2 CUPS LONG-GRAIN RICE, PREFERABLY JASMINE

2 1/2 CUPS CHICKEN OR VEGETABLE STOCK

SALT AND FRESHLY GROUND BLACK PEPPER, TO TASTE

6 TO 8 SERVINGS

Heat the oil in a heavy 3-quart saucepan. Add the onion and ginger and sauté over medium-low heat until the onion is translucent. Stir in the dry mustard, then add the rice. Stir again.

Add the stock, bring to a simmer, season with salt and pepper, and then cover and cook over very low heat until the liquid has been absorbed and the rice is tender, about 15 minutes. Set aside, covered, for 10 minutes. Check seasoning and add more salt and pepper if needed. Toss gently to fluff the rice, and serve.

Rice can be a challenge for many cooks. One trick that it pays to remember when you are cooking a pilaf (that is, a recipe that calls for all the liquid to be absorbed by the rice) is to let it sit, covered, for 10 minutes after the cooking has been completed. It will make all the difference in the texture.

Timbales of Smashed Garlic Potatoes

THIS RECIPE WAS A HAPPY ACCIDENT. I HAD MADE A LARGE BATCH OF MASHED RED POTATOES, DONE WITHOUT PEELING THEM, AND I HAD PUT THE LEFTOVERS IN A COUPLE OF PORCELAIN RAMEKINS AND REFRIGERATED THEM OVERNIGHT. THE NEXT DAY I HEATED THE POTATOES RIGHT IN THE OVENPROOF RAMEKINS AND THEN UNMOLDED THEM. I LOVED THE WAY THEY CAME OUT, SO I FINE-TUNED THE RECIPE A BIT, BOUGHT A BUNCH OF NON-STICK RAMEKINS, AND NOW I ALWAYS SERVE MASHED RED POTATOES THIS WAY. YOU CAN EITHER PUT A SERVING ON EACH DINNER PLATE OR ARRANGE THE UNMOLDED POTATOES ON A PLATTER.

1 1/2 POUNDS SMALL RED POTATOES

SALT

6 TABLESPOONS UNSALTED BUTTER, SOFTENED

2 TABLESPOONS WHOLE MILK OR HALF-AND-HALF

4 CLOVES GARLIC, MASHED

FRESHLY GROUND BLACK PEPPER, TO TASTE

1/2 CUP FINELY CHOPPED FLAT-LEAF PARSLEY LEAVES, PLUS 4 SPRIGS FOR GARNISH

Place the potatoes in a saucepan, add salted water, bring to a boil, and simmer until tender. Drain the potatoes and transfer to a large, clean, smooth dish towel (not terry cloth). Wrap the potatoes in the towel and smash them with a rolling pin, a meat pounder or a big wooden spoon. Remove the potatoes from the towel and place them in a bowl.

Preheat the oven to 350 degrees. Use 2 tablespoons of the butter to heavily grease four 8-ounce ovenproof ramekins.

Place the remaining butter in a small saucepan with the milk and garlic over low heat. When the butter has melted, pour the contents of the saucepan over the potatoes in the bowl and mix thoroughly. Fold in the parsley and season to taste with salt and pepper.

Pack the potatoes in the ramekins and place in the oven. Bake for 30 minutes, until heated through and starting to crisp around the edges.

Run a knife around the outside edges of the ramekins to loosen the potatoes. Invert each ramekin onto a dinner plate and lift off the ramekin. Garnish with a sprig of parsley.

Smashing the potatoes in a towel is an extremely effective way to achieve the perfect texture for these potatoes. It yields a drier mash, allowing the potatoes to more fully absorb the butter, milk, and garlic, and keeps the texture appealingly rough.

Although it takes a little longer, plucking the leaves off the parsley sprigs and using only the leaves is worth the effort—and a sure sign of a well-schooled chef.

HEDVIG HRICAK, M.D.

Swiss Chard and Potatoes

Bitva is the name for Swiss chard in Croatia. Along the Dalmatian coast, it is usually served with simple, grilled fresh fish. That is how we serve it during the summer at our vacation house in Croatia. Even when I eat Swiss chard elsewhere, I think of warm summer evenings on the Dalmatian coast.

2 pounds Swiss chard

1 1/2 pounds medium-size Yukon Gold potatoes

1/4 cup extra virgin olive oil

3 cloves garlic, peeled and sliced thin

Salt and freshly ground black pepper, to taste

Swiss chard comes in a rainbow of colors these days: with red, yellow, and orange stems in addition to the more common white. You can use a mixture in this recipe. The best way to remove the stems is to fold the leaves in half lengthwise, along the stem, and then slice out the stems. Though the stems are not usually included in this dish, there is no reason why they couldn't be, to add a bit of nice texture.

Rinse the Swiss chard well, trim and discard the bottom half-inch from the stems, and then remove the stems. Tear the leaves into large pieces and dice the stems. Peel the potatoes and dice them into ½-inch cubes.

Bring a large pot of water to a boil, add the chard leaves and stems and the potatoes, and cook until just tender, about 10 minutes. Drain well.

Heat the olive oil in a large skillet and add the garlic. Sauté until the garlic barely begins to turn golden, then add the drained Swiss chard and potatoes. Stir, add salt and pepper to taste, cook for about a minute, and then serve.

Gramma Betty's Favorite Stuffed Potatoes

THIS IS THE WAY POTATOES WERE ALWAYS SERVED AT MY GRANDMOTHER'S HOUSE. THE MENU WOULD BE ROAST LOIN OF PORK, GREEN BEANS, THESE POTATOES, AND A SALAD WITH ITALIAN DRESSING. GRAMMA BETTY WOULD SEE TO IT THAT THERE WOULD BE ENOUGH OF HER GREAT GRAVY FROM THE PORK TO DRIZZLE OVER THE POTATOES. THE BEST PART OF THIS DISH, FOR THE HOST OR HOSTESS, IS THAT THE POTATOES CAN BE MADE WELL IN ADVANCE AND THEN PUT IN THE OVEN TO BAKE SHORTLY BEFORE DINNER IS READY. ONCE THE BAKING IS FINISHED, THEY CAN BE KEPT WARM IN A LOW OVEN (ABOUT 200 DEGREES) FOR UP TO ONE HOUR.

4 LARGE BAKING POTATOES, SCRUBBED

1/2 CUP SOUR CREAM OR WHOLE MILK YOGURT

3 TABLESPOONS UNSALTED BUTTER, SOFTENED

1/4 CUP WARM MILK

2 TABLESPOONS MINCED CHIVES

SALT AND FRESHLY GROUND BLACK PEPPER

1/2 CUP GRATED SHARP WHITE CHEDDAR CHEESE, ABOUT 2 OUNCES

8 SERVINGS

Preheat the oven to 400 degrees. Bake the potatoes for 40 to 60 minutes, until the point of a knife or a thin skewer meets no resistance. Remove the potatoes from the oven. Reduce the oven temperature to 350 degrees.

Cut each potato in half lengthwise and scoop out the flesh into a bowl, taking care not to break the skin.

Mash the potatoes with the sour cream or yogurt, the butter, milk, and chives until the mixture is smooth. Season to taste with salt and pepper. Pack the potato mixture back in the skins, smooth the tops, and place on a baking sheet. Sprinkle the tops of the potatoes with the cheese.

Return the potatoes to the oven for about 30 minutes, until the cheese is melted and the tops are starting to brown. Serve.

Instead of topping the potatoes with cheese, serve them with a choice of toppings in small bowls: sour cream and chives, crumbled blue cheese mixed with sour cream, crumbled crisp bacon, and diced sautéed mushrooms.

THE SWEET LIFE

Sour Cream Chocolate Cake

Alane's Mexican Chocolate Cake

Crowd-Pleasing Sour Cream Walnut Cake

Coker Family Pound Cake

Rhubarb Cake

Blueberry Cake

Pumpkin Cheesecake

Texas Pecan Pie

Dutch Baby with Strawberries

Adult Applesauce

Petit Pots de Crème au Chocolat

Bermuda Banana Pudding

Baked Rice Pudding

Strawberry Soufflé

Chocolate Soufflé

My Mother's Pavlova

Lemon Squares

Aunt Julie's Sugar-Crusted Brownies

Millionaire Turtles

Coconut Macaroons

Chocolate Chip Cinnamon Oatmeal Cookies

My Nanny Anna's Crescent Cookies

Vera's Farina Halvah

Panda Bear Cupcakes

Left: Petits Pots de Crème au Chocolat

Sour Cream Chocolate Cake

THIS IS A RECIPE THAT CAME TO ME FROM BERMUDA, AND I HAVE EVEN BEEN SERVED IT IN LONDON. IT'S A RICH CHOCOLATE CAKE THAT FREEZES REALLY WELL AND LOOKS AS GOOD AS IT TASTES. SERVE IT ON YOUR PRETTIEST CAKE STAND, WITH A SILVER SERVER.

4 TABLESPOONS UNSALTED BUTTER, SOFTENED, PLUS BUTTER FOR PANS

2 CUPS ALL-PURPOSE FLOUR, PLUS MORE FOR PANS

6 OUNCES HIGH-QUALITY UNSWEETENED CHOCOLATE (99 PERCENT CACAO)

1 1/4 TEASPOONS BAKING SODA

1/2 TEASPOON BAKING POWDER

1 TEASPOON SALT

1 2/3 CUPS GRANULATED SUGAR

2 LARGE EGGS

3/4 CUP SOUR CREAM

1 TEASPOON VANILLA EXTRACT

CHOCOLATE SOUR CREAM FROSTING:

6 TABLESPOONS UNSALTED BUTTER, IN PIECES

4 OUNCES HIGH-QUALITY UNSWEETENED CHOCOLATE (99 PERCENT CACAO)

3 CUPS CONFECTIONERS' SUGAR

1/2 CUP SOUR CREAM

1 1/2 TEASPOONS VANILLA EXTRACT

8 SERVINGS

Preheat the oven to 350 degrees. Butter and flour two 9-inch round layer-cake pans.

Break up the 6 ounces of chocolate and place it in a saucepan with 1 cup of water. Cook over very low heat just until the chocolate melts. Set aside. In a bowl, whisk together the 2 cups of flour, the baking soda, baking powder, and salt.

Beat the 4 tablespoons butter with the granulated sugar until creamy. Beat in the eggs, one at a time. Stir in the chocolate mixture and the sour cream. Stir in the flour mixture and add the vanilla.

Pour the batter into the prepared pans and bake about 25 minutes, until a cake tester comes out clean. Allow the layers to cool on racks in their pans for 20 minutes, then remove them from the pans to continue cooling on racks.

When the layers have cooled completely, melt the butter and chocolate for the frosting in a heavy saucepan over very low heat. Remove from heat, transfer to a large metal bowl placed in a large bowl of ice water to cool it. Whisk in the confectioners' sugar, and then blend in the sour cream and vanilla. Beat until smooth. Spread icing on tops of both layers, stack them, then ice the sides.

Melting the chocolate in water or butter is foolproof. The chocolate cannot burn, and there is enough water or butter so it will not tighten up as it might in contact with just a little liquid. Be sure to use a high-quality unsweetened chocolate.

SALLIE GIORDANO

Alane's Mexican Chocolate Cake

*T*HIS IS AN OLD SOUTHERN RECIPE THAT SHOWS UP TIME AND AGAIN.
MY VERSION COMES FROM MY SISTER-IN-LAW, ALANE FOSTER. ITS MEXICAN
CONNECTION IS THE ADDITION OF CINNAMON TO THE CHOCOLATE.
WITHOUT THE CINNAMON, THE CAKE IS SIMPLY A FINE OLD-FASHIONED CHOCOLATE CAKE.

¼ POUND PLUS 4 TABLESPOONS (1½ STICKS) UNSALTED BUTTER,
IN PIECES, PLUS MORE FOR PAN

2 CUPS ALL-PURPOSE FLOUR, PLUS MORE FOR PAN

2 CUPS GRANULATED SUGAR

1 TEASPOON BAKING SODA

6 TABLESPOONS UNSWEETENED COCOA, PREFERABLY DUTCH PROCESS

½ CUP BUTTERMILK

2 LARGE EGGS

1 TEASPOON CINNAMON

1 TEASPOON VANILLA EXTRACT

CINNAMON-CHOCOLATE FROSTING:

6 TABLESPOONS UNSALTED BUTTER

4 TABLESPOONS UNSWEETENED COCOA, PREFERABLY DUTCH PROCESS

4 TABLESPOONS BUTTERMILK

2 CUPS CONFECTIONERS' SUGAR

½ TEASPOON CINNAMON

PINCH OF SALT

1 CUP COARSELY CHOPPED PECANS OR TOASTED PINE NUTS, OPTIONAL

24 SERVINGS

Preheat the oven to 375 degrees. Butter and flour a baking pan, 9 x 13 inches.

Whisk the 2 cups flour, the granulated sugar, and baking soda together in a large bowl.

In a small saucepan, bring the 1½ sticks of butter, the cocoa powder, and 1 cup of water just to a simmer until the butter melts. Whisk to blend.

Mix the buttermilk, eggs, cinnamon, and vanilla in another bowl.

Pour the hot butter mixture into the flour mixture and beat just until blended. Add the egg mixture and beat it in. Pour the batter into the prepared pan and bake for 25 to 30 minutes or until a toothpick inserted into the middle comes out clean.

Remove from the oven and let cool on a rack.

For the frosting, combine the butter, cocoa, buttermilk, confectioners' sugar, cinnamon, and salt in a saucepan. Bring to a simmer, just until the butter melts. Beat until smooth. Transfer the mixture to a metal bowl placed in a larger bowl of ice and water and let cool for about 10 minutes, stirring from time to time. Pour the frosting over the cooled cake and spread it. If desired, scatter the nuts on top.

*Squares of this cake make a fine accompaniment for ice cream
or sorbet and would be a delicious addition to afternoon tea.
If you unmold the cake before icing it, you can turn it into a
birthday cake for a crowd.*

Crowd–Pleasing Sour Cream Walnut Cake

*I*HAVE NO RECOLLECTION WHERE I FOUND THIS RECIPE, BUT IT WAS A WHILE AGO. I ENJOY IT BECAUSE IT IS EASY TO MAKE AND DELICIOUS! I CAN RELY ON IT TO USE FOR CHURCH FELLOWSHIP, BAKE SALES, OR AS A HOSTESS GIFT WHEN I AM INVITED TO DINNER. PEOPLE ALL SEEM TO ENJOY IT. VANILLA ICE CREAM IS ABOUT THE ONLY EMBELLISHMENT IT MIGHT NEED. I MADE ONE FOR THE ANNUAL NEW YEAR'S EVE PARTY FOR OUR PATIENTS AND THEIR FAMILIES. IT DISAPPEARED RAPIDLY, AND ONE LADY WAS SO TAKEN WITH IT THAT SHE ASKED ME TO E-MAIL HER THE RECIPE. AND IT WAS NOT THE FIRST TIME I HAD GOTTEN A REQUEST LIKE THAT!

6½ TABLESPOONS PLUS ¼ POUND UNSALTED BUTTER, SOFTENED

2 CUPS ALL-PURPOSE FLOUR, PLUS MORE FOR PAN

2 TEASPOONS CINNAMON

I CUP LIGHT BROWN SUGAR

¾ CUP CHOPPED WALNUTS OR PECANS

I TEASPOON BAKING SODA

I TEASPOON BAKING POWDER

I TEASPOON SALT

I½ CUPS RAISINS

¾ CUP GRANULATED SUGAR

I TEASPOON VANILLA EXTRACT

3 LARGE EGGS

I CUP SOUR CREAM OR WHOLE MILK YOGURT

12 SERVINGS

Use 1 tablespoon of the butter to grease a 9- or 10-inch tube pan or Bundt pan. Dust with flour. Preheat the oven to 350 degrees.

In a small bowl, mix the cinnamon, brown sugar, and nuts together. Using a fork or your fingertips, work 5½ tablespoons of the butter into this mixture, until it becomes somewhat crumbly. Set it aside. In another bowl, whisk the 2 cups of flour with the baking soda, baking powder, and salt. Stir in the raisins. Set aside.

Beat the remaining stick of butter and the granulated sugar together, by hand or machine, until fluffy. Beat in the vanilla. Beat in the eggs, one at a time. Add the dry ingredients to the egg mixture alternately with the sour cream.

Spread one-third of the batter into the prepared pan. Sprinkle with half the nut mixture. Add another third of the batter, and then the rest of the nut mixture and the remaining batter.

Bake for 50 minutes. Cool 10 minutes in the pan; then remove from the pan and continue cooling.

Since removing a cake from most tube pans involves inverting it and serving it bottom side up, the recipe is best made with the nut mixture in layers within the batter, as indicated here. However, if you have a springform tube pan that permits the cake to be removed without inverting, it, you can spread half the batter in the pan, then half the nut mixture, the remaining batter and finally the rest of the nut mixture, which will become a crunchy topping.

JIMMIE HOLLAND, M.D.

Coker Family Pound Cake

Three generations of my Texas family have enjoyed this simple yellow cake. It's entirely likely that the cake originally came from Mississippi and from Scotland before that. Pound cake refers to the old-fashioned recipes that were made with a pound of butter, a pound of sugar, and a pound of flour. We've adjusted those proportions a bit.

½ pound (2 sticks) unsalted butter

3 cups all-purpose flour

1 teaspoon salt

½ teaspoon baking soda

½ teaspoon ground mace

2 cups granulated sugar

6 large eggs

1 cup buttermilk

1 teaspoon vanilla extract

Confectioners' sugar for dusting

12 servings

Preheat the oven to 350 degrees. Use a little of the butter to grease a 9- or 10-inch Bundt or tube pan. Dust with a little of the flour.

Whisk the remaining flour with the salt, baking soda, and mace in a large bowl.

Using an electric mixer, cream the remaining butter with the granulated sugar. Beat in the eggs one at a time. Mix the buttermilk with the vanilla and add it in three parts, alternately with the flour mixture, ending with the flour.

Pour into the prepared pan and bake about 1 hour, until a cake tester comes out clean.

Cool in the pan, then unmold. Dust the cake with sifted confectioners' sugar before serving.

Pound cake is a blank slate. But it doesn't take much to dress it up: Fresh strawberries in summer, a compote of stewed dried fruits or apples and quince in winter. Whipped cream or ice cream would be perfect alongside. The cake can be baked in two 8-inch loaf pans instead of a single Bundt pan, depending on your presentation.

Rhubarb Cake

My grandmother grew rhubarb in her garden, and she would always pick it fresh for this cake. At the end of the season, she even froze some of the last of the rhubarb so we could have this cake later on. It's perfect for a picnic or a casual dinner party with vanilla ice cream. Fresh rhubarb really makes this cake. However, when rhubarb is not available, tart chunks of apple or even of quince offer fine substitutes.

¼ pound (1 stick) unsalted butter

1½ cups light brown sugar

2 large eggs

2 cups all-purpose flour

1 teaspoon baking soda

½ teaspoon salt

1 cup sour milk, buttermilk, or plain lowfat yogurt

1 teaspoon vanilla extract

2 cups fresh rhubarb (about 3 medium-size stalks), diced

⅓ cup granulated sugar

½ teaspoon cinnamon

12 to 16 servings

Preheat the oven to 350 degrees. Use a little of the butter to grease a baking pan, 9 x 13 inches.

Cream the remaining butter and the brown sugar. Beat in the eggs, one at a time.

Whisk the flour, baking soda, and salt together in a bowl and add it to the brown sugar mixture alternately with the sour milk. Stir in the vanilla. Fold in the rhubarb.

Mix the granulated sugar and the cinnamon together in a small bowl.

Spread the batter in the pan. Sprinkle with the cinnamon sugar. Bake about 35 minutes, until a cake tester comes out clean. Allow the cake to cool in the pan before cutting in squares and transferring to a platter.

Another way to serve the cake is to skip the dusting of cinnamon-sugar before baking and sift confectioners' sugar over the cake after it has cooled.

Blueberry Cake

*T*HIS CAKE IS UNUSUAL. IT IS MADE WITHOUT EGGS. EVERY SUMMER MY SISTER AND I BAKE IT WHEN THE BLUEBERRIES ARE IN SEASON AT LOCAL FARMS NEAR OUR HOUSE IN SOUTHAMPTON. SOMETIMES WE USE PEACHES INSTEAD OF BLUEBERRIES. DUST THE TOP OF THIS CAKE WITH A LITTLE CINNAMON-SUGAR BEFORE BAKING AND YOU CAN SERVE IT FOR A WEEKEND BREAKFAST. BUT THEN, GOOD, THICK YOGURT INSTEAD OF ICE CREAM SHOULD GO ALONGSIDE.

6 TABLESPOONS UNSALTED BUTTER

1 CUP ALL-PURPOSE FLOUR

1 CUP SUGAR

1 TABLESPOON BAKING POWDER

3/4 CUP MILK

2 CUPS BLUEBERRIES

VANILLA ICE CREAM, FOR SERVING

Preheat the oven to 350 degrees.

Place the butter in a rectangular baking dish, about 9 x 13 inches, preferably heat-proof glass. Place the dish in the oven until the butter melts.

Meanwhile, whisk together the flour, sugar, and baking powder in a bowl. Stir in the milk just until the ingredients are moistened. Do not expect a smooth batter.

When the butter has melted, remove the baking dish from the oven and pour the batter in it, tilting the dish to spread the batter over the bottom.

Spoon the berries evenly on top.

Place in the oven and bake about 45 minutes, until lightly browned. Serve while still warm.

8 SERVINGS

Pumpkin Cheesecake

HERE IS A CAKE THAT IS DECADENT BUT DELICIOUS AND WELL WORTH THE CALORIES. BESIDES, IT IS EASY TO MAKE. IS THERE A MORE PERFECT FALL DESSERT?

4½ tablespoons unsalted butter, melted

1½ cups graham cracker crumbs

½ cup granulated sugar

½ teaspoon ground cloves

4 packages (8 ounces each) cream cheese, softened

1 cup firmly packed light brown sugar

5 eggs

¼ cup all-purpose flour

1 can (16 ounces) unseasoned pumpkin puree

1 teaspoon ground ginger

½ teaspoon grated nutmeg

Pinch of salt

Sifted confectioners' sugar, for serving

12 TO 16 SERVINGS

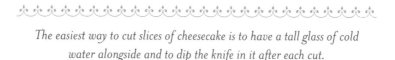

The easiest way to cut slices of cheesecake is to have a tall glass of cold water alongside and to dip the knife in it after each cut.

Preheat the oven to 350 degrees. Use ½ tablespoon of the butter to grease the sides of a 9-inch springform pan.

Mix the crumbs with the granulated sugar and ¼ teaspoon of the cloves in a bowl. Use a fork to stir in the remaining melted butter to coat the crumbs. Press the crumbs in the bottom and about an inch up the sides of the baking pan.

In the bowl of an electric mixer, beat the cream cheese at medium speed using the paddle attachment until smooth and creamy. Gradually beat in the 1 cup light brown sugar until the mixture is smooth. At low speed, beat in the eggs one at a time until just blended. Beat in the flour, the pumpkin, and the remaining seasonings. Mix well.

Pour the filling into the graham cracker crust.

Bake about 1 hour 15 minutes. The cake may crack a bit. Turn the oven off and open the oven door a little. Let the cheesecake sit in the oven for 30 minutes. Remove the cheesecake from the oven and continue cooling on a wire rack for 30 to 45 minutes, then refrigerate covered with foil. Before serving, cover the cracks on the top with a dusting of confectioners' sugar.

NOTE: If you use canned pumpkin, be sure it is unsweetened and unseasoned. Plain frozen butternut squash, or homemade butternut squash puree are two alternatives.

Texas Pecan Pie

PECAN PIE IS A MUST ON TEXAN HOLIDAY TABLES. THIS RECIPE COMES FROM MY MOTHER'S FAMILY. WHEN SERVING A DESSERT LIKE THIS, CUT MERE SLIVERS FOR THE LADIES. THEY WILL APPRECIATE THE GESTURE AND MAY EVEN ASK FOR SECONDS.

3/4 CUP SUGAR

I TABLESPOON ALL-PURPOSE FLOUR

I CUP LIGHT CORN SYRUP

2 TABLESPOONS UNSALTED BUTTER

3 LARGE EGGS

I TEASPOON VANILLA EXTRACT

PINCH OF SALT

1 1/2 CUP PECANS, COARSELY CHOPPED OR HALVES

BAKED BASIC PIE OR TART PASTRY (RECIPE FOLLOWS),
OR A 9-INCH UNBAKED PIE SHELL

SOFTLY WHIPPED CREAM OR VANILLA ICE CREAM FOR SERVING

Preheat the oven to 325 degrees.

Place the sugar in a small saucepan and whisk in the flour. Whisk in the syrup and add the butter. Heat just until the butter melts and the sugar has dissolved.

In a large bowl, lightly beat the eggs, just enough to break them up and amalgamate them. They must not become frothy. Very slowly whisk the heated sugar and syrup mixture into the eggs, mixing constantly. Stir in the vanilla, salt, and pecans.

Pour the mixture into the pie or tart shell, place in the oven, and bake about 45 minutes, until the top is firm. It will puff up somewhat and then sink down.

Allow to cool at least 1 hour before cutting. Serve with whipped cream or ice cream.

BAKED BASIC PIE OR TART PASTRY

ONE 8- OR 9-INCH PIE OR TART SHELL

1 ½ CUPS ALL-PURPOSE FLOUR, PLUS MORE FOR ROLLING

½ TEASPOON SALT

6 TABLESPOONS UNSALTED BUTTER, CHILLED AND DICED

1 EGG YOLK BEATEN WITH 3 TABLESPOONS COLD WATER

Preheat the oven to 425 degrees.

Whirl the flour and salt together in a food processor. Add the butter and pulse until the mixture is crumbly. Open the container and sprinkle the egg yolk mixture in. Pulse about a dozen times, until a dough comes together. If the mixture is too dry, sprinkle in a little more water and pulse a few times again.

Gather the dough into a ball, flatten it, wrap it in plastic, and refrigerate it for 30 minutes. Roll out the dough on a floured board to a round large enough to fit into a 9-inch pie pan or an 8-inch straight-sided tart pan. Line the pan with foil and baking weights or dried beans. Bake for 10 minutes, until the pastry starts to look dry. Remove the foil and weights and bake 10 minutes more, until the pasty is lightly golden. Remove from the oven.

The pastry is rich yet not sweet, and can be used for all sorts of recipes, from savory quiches to sweet desserts, like this pecan pie. Baking in a straight-sided French tart pan instead of an American pie plate allows you to remove the sides of the pan for a prettier presentation. Baking the pastry before filling will guarantee that the crust will not become soggy after its second baking with the filling.

KELLY FORSBERG

Dutch Baby with Strawberries

THIS CRÊPELIKE PANCAKE THAT YOU BAKE IN THE OVEN IS GREAT FOR BREAKFAST BUT CAN ALSO BE USED FOR A DESSERT. THE RECIPE WAS GIVEN TO ME BY AN OLD FRIEND FROM COLLEGE, AND IT WAS IN HER FAMILY FOR GENERATIONS. SHE SERVED THIS TO MY HUSBAND AND ME WHEN WE VISITED HER.

1 PINT STRAWBERRIES, HULLED AND SLICED

1/2 CUP SUGAR, APPROXIMATELY

1/4 POUND (1 STICK) UNSALTED BUTTER

3 EGGS

1 CUP ALL-PURPOSE FLOUR

1 TEASPOON SALT

1 1/2 CUPS MILK

1/2 TEASPOON VANILLA EXTRACT

4 TO 6 SERVINGS

Sweeten strawberries to taste with about ¼ cup of the sugar. Set aside.

Preheat the oven to 400 degrees.

Place the butter in a 10-inch cast-iron skillet, and place the skillet in the oven until the butter melts.

Meanwhile, mix the eggs, remaining sugar, flour, salt, milk, and vanilla in a blender or food processor until smooth.

As soon as the butter has melted, pour the egg mixture into the skillet, tipping it to spread the batter evenly. Return the skillet to the oven and bake until puffed and browned, about 25 minutes.

Cut the puffed pancake in wedges and serve with strawberries.

Call this comfort food. Just as some professional chefs serve a version of French toast as a dessert, there is no reason why this pancake, which is terrific at brunch, can't also go on the dessert table. However, there is no substitute for bringing the skillet right to the table straight from the oven. Just be sure to have a good heatproof trivet ready. (If you don't have a cast-iron skillet on hand, a 10-inch pie pan will also work.)

Adult Applesauce

I FIRST CONCOCTED THIS RECIPE ON A FALL WEEKEND WHEN WE WERE UP IN OUR HOUSE IN ROCHESTER, VERMONT. WE HAD LOTS OF APPLES. WHAT TO DO WITH THEM? WITH LEMON JUICE AND RUM, THIS IS DEFINITELY NOT APPLESAUCE FOR THE CHILDREN. WHILE YOU'RE AT IT, SPOON THE APPLESAUCE INTO WINE GOBLETS TO GIVE THE DESSERT A TRULY GROWN-UP PRESENTATION.

12 TART RED APPLES

JUICE OF 2 LEMONS

1 1/2 CUPS RAISINS

3/4 CUP DARK RUM

1/2 CUP LIGHT BROWN SUGAR

SOFTLY WHIPPED CREAM OR CRÈME FRAÎCHE, OPTIONAL

FRESHLY GRATED NUTMEG

6 SERVINGS

Cut the apples in eighths, skins, seeds, and all. Place them in a heavy saucepan with 2 cups water and the lemon juice. Bring to a simmer and cook over low heat, covered, about 45 minutes, until the apples are very soft.

Meanwhile, place the raisins in a small bowl, add the rum, and set aside.

Transfer the apples to a large, coarse sieve over a bowl and force them through, or place them in a food mill and process.

Return the strained applesauce to the saucepan, add the sugar, rum, and the raisins. Simmer, stirring occasionally, for about 10 minutes, just until the sugar dissolves. Serve warm, at room temperature, or chilled, topped, if desired, with a little cloud of cream dusted with nutmeg.

You can use a mixture of apples, not just one kind, for this applesauce. It will add complexity to the flavor. Calvados or applejack can be used in place of the rum.

Petits Pots de Crème au Chocolat

THIS IS A STREAMLINED VERSION OF MY MOTHER'S PARISIAN RECIPE FOR A DESSERT THAT WAS ALWAYS A SUCCESS AT HER DINNER PARTIES IN CALIFORNIA. I STARTED MAKING IT ABOUT THIRTY YEARS AGO IN NEW YORK. THIS RECIPE HAS TRAVELED! BUT I STREAMLINED IT. INSTEAD OF BAKING THE CUSTARD IN A BAIN-MARIE, I DO THE WHOLE THING IN A BLENDER. THE HOT CREAM COOKS THE EGGS TO THICKEN THE CUSTARD. THE END RESULT IS NEARLY IDENTICAL TO THE ORIGINAL. I SOMETIMES VARY THE RECIPE BY ADDING A LITTLE COGNAC, POIRE WILLIAMS OR FRAMBOISE EAU-DE-VIE, OR COINTREAU, OR EVEN SOME STRONG COFFEE.

1 POUND HIGH-QUALITY BITTERSWEET CHOCOLATE (ABOUT 70 PERCENT CACAO),
BROKEN IN SMALL PIECES

1 TEASPOON VANILLA EXTRACT

PINCH OF SALT

1 TABLESPOON LIQUEUR OR OTHER FLAVORING, OPTIONAL

6 LARGE EGG YOLKS

2 CUPS HEAVY CREAM

8 TO 10 SERVINGS

Place the chocolate, vanilla, and salt, and liqueur if using, in a food processor and pulse to mix and break up the chocolate. Add the egg yolks and process briefly to mix.

Place 1½ cups of the cream in a heavy saucepan and bring to a boil. Pour the cream into the food processor and process until well blended, scraping the sides of the bowl at least once.

Pour into pots de crème cups, demi-tasse cups, ramekins, or small wine glasses and chill until ready to serve.

Whip remaining cream and top each serving with a dollop of it.

NOTE: The hot cream is enough to cook the egg yolks. But if you have concerns about using raw egg yolks without fully cooking them, then you should use organic eggs, as the risk of salmonella contamination is dramatically reduced. Also, you can purchase pasteurized egg yolks.

The recipe calls for bittersweet chocolate, but semisweet would also be good. And for another variation, use milk chocolate and add a tablespoon of malt powder to the mixture. Another possibility would be to use white chocolate and either white crème de cacao or white crème de menthe. For a buffet dinner, you can double the recipe and chill the custard on Chinese porcelain soup spoons and then pass them on a tray. You will have 24 servings this way.

Bermuda Banana Pudding

*T*HIS IS A CLASSIC BERMUDA RECIPE. IT IS SOMETIMES MADE WITH LOCALLY GROWN BERMUDA BANANAS, WHICH ARE NOT AS SWEET AS CENTRAL AMERICAN ONES. FOR A REAL BERMUDA TOUCH, OFFER SMALL SNIFTERS OF AGED RUM TO SIP ALONGSIDE THE PUDDING.

6 TABLESPOONS UNSALTED BUTTER

2 CUPS PLAIN BREAD CRUMBS

4 LARGE EGGS

1½ CUPS MILK

1 CUP SUGAR

1 TEASPOON VANILLA EXTRACT

6 LARGE BANANAS, JUST RIPE

3 LARGE EGG WHITES

PINCH OF CREAM OF TARTAR

8 TO 10 SERVINGS

Preheat the oven to 350 degrees. Use a tablespoon of the butter to grease a 2-quart oblong baking dish.

Melt the remaining butter in a small skillet. Toss the bread crumbs with the butter and cook over low heat until the crumbs are golden.

In a bowl, beat the whole eggs, milk, ½ cup of the sugar, and the vanilla together until well blended.

Cut the bananas in slices about ¼ inch thick. Arrange a layer of the bananas in the bottom of the dish. Sprinkle them with one-third of the bread crumbs. Repeat the layers, ending with the bread crumbs. Pour the egg mixture over and around the ingredients in the dish. Place in the oven and bake 25 minutes.

As soon as the baking time is up, turn off the oven, leaving the dish inside while you beat the egg whites with the cream of tartar until very softly peaked. Gradually beat in the remaining sugar.

Remove the baking dish from the oven and spoon or pipe on the egg whites to cover the top. Return the dish to the oven and bake another 15 minutes, until the top is starting to brown.

Allow the pudding to cool briefly and then serve.

This recipe amounts to a bread pudding with bananas and meringue. But because of the meringue, it's important to serve the pudding soon after it has finished baking.

Baked Rice Pudding

*I*N OUR HOUSE, HOLIDAYS WOULD NOT BE THE SAME WITHOUT THIS RICE PUDDING; WE ALWAYS SERVE IT WITH THE MEAL. WHEN IT IS SERVED ON CHRISTMAS EVE, ACCORDING TO SWEDISH LORE, AN ALMOND IS PUT INSIDE THE PUDDING AND THE ONE WHO GETS IT IS SAID TO MARRY WITHIN THE YEAR. TRADITIONALLY, A LINGONBERRY SAUCE GOES ALONGSIDE THE PUDDING. JARRED LINGONBERRIES ARE SOLD IN FINE FOOD SHOPS AND ONLINE. RASPBERRY PUREE, SWEETENED TO TASTE, IS A FINE ALTERNATIVE.

3/4 CUP LONG GRAIN RICE

1/2 TEASPOON SALT

2 CUPS MILK

2/3 CUP SUGAR

1/2 CUP HEAVY CREAM

1 TABLESPOON UNSALTED BUTTER, SOFTENED

2 LARGE EGGS

1 TEASPOON VANILLA EXTRACT

1/2 TEASPOON NUTMEG, PREFERABLY FRESHLY GRATED

8 TO 10 SERVINGS

Place the rice in a 2-quart saucepan, add 2 cups water, and simmer, covered, until the water is nearly absorbed and the rice is tender, about 15 minutes. Add the milk and the sugar and cook about 5 minutes. Remove from heat. Stir in the cream.

Preheat the oven to 350 degrees. Butter a 2-quart baking dish or soufflé dish. Set the dish in a roasting pan that will hold it comfortably.

Beat the eggs in a large bowl until well blended. Gradually fold the rice mixture into the eggs and add the vanilla. Pour into the baking dish. Dust with the nutmeg.

Place in the oven and pour boiling water into the roasting pan so it comes halfway up the sides of the baking dish. Bake about 1 hour, until a knife inserted in the center comes out nearly clean.

Allow to cool before serving.

Another way to prepare this pudding, without baking it, is to allow the rice, milk, cream, and sugar mixture to cool completely, then refrigerate it. Just before serving, fold in 2 cups of heavy cream, whipped.

Strawberry Soufflé

*M*Y GRANDMOTHER, WHO WAS NOT A GOOD COOK, HAD A LIMITED REPERTORY THAT INCLUDED A FEW WINNERS, LIKE THIS VERY SIMPLE, FRESH-TASTING SOUFFLÉ. PLAN ON MAKING IT WHEN FRESH STRAWBERRIES ARE IN SEASON.

1 PINT FRESH STRAWBERRIES, HULLED

⅓ CUP PLUS 3 TABLESPOONS GRANULATED SUGAR

2 TABLESPOONS KIRSCH, OPTIONAL

1 TABLESPOON UNSALTED BUTTER, SOFTENED

3 LARGE EGG WHITES, AT ROOM TEMPERATURE

PINCH OF CREAM OF TARTAR

1 TABLESPOON CONFECTIONERS' SUGAR

Pulse the strawberries in a food processor until finely chopped. Sweeten them with ⅓ cup sugar and stir in the kirsch, if using. Set aside.

Preheat the oven to 300 degrees. Butter a 1-quart soufflé dish and dust it with 1½ tablespoons of the sugar. Set the dish in a larger pan. Have a kettle of boiling water ready.

Beat the egg whites with the cream of tartar until softly peaked. Continue beating while gradually adding the remaining 1½ tablespoons sugar, beating until the egg whites are stiff. Gently fold in the strawberries.

Place in the oven and add boiling water to the larger pan to come about halfway up the sides of the baking dish. Bake about 25 minutes, until puffed and firm on top.

Sift the confectioners' sugar over the top and serve.

4 SERVINGS

This is a simple egg white soufflé. It is not as rich as a traditional
soufflé made with a custard base. You can puree additional
strawberries and sweeten them to use as a sauce.

Chocolate Soufflé

My husband, Derek Limbocker, is the one who takes the bows when our guests are served this soufflé. He does all the work. This is as dramatic and impressive as a dessert can be. It's an enormous soufflé and must be served as soon as it comes out of the oven. Have your dessert plates at your elbow, bring out the soufflé, and dish it out to the guests at your dinner table without delay. Pass softly whipped cream alongside.

¼ POUND (1 STICK) UNSALTED BUTTER, SOFTENED

1 CUP PLUS 2 TABLESPOONS GRANULATED SUGAR

4 TABLESPOONS ALL-PURPOSE FLOUR

8 OUNCES HIGH-QUALITY SEMISWEET CHOCOLATE
(65 TO 70 PERCENT CACAO), CHOPPED

2 CUPS MILK, SCALDED

8 LARGE EGG YOLKS

1½ TEASPOONS VANILLA EXTRACT

12 LARGE EGG WHITES, AT ROOM TEMPERATURE

1½ TEASPOONS CREAM OF TARTAR

1½ TABLESPOONS CONFECTIONERS' SUGAR

*Fine chocolate in bars is usually sold according to its cacao content.
A percentage of around 65 to 75 percent indicates that the chocolate
is semisweet or bittersweet. There is no official standard to explain the
difference between semisweet and bittersweet.*

8 TO 10 SERVINGS

Prepare a 3-quart soufflé dish. Use 1½ tablespoons butter to grease the dish. Take a strip of aluminum foil, 8 inches wide and long enough to wrap the circumference of the dish with an overlap, and fold it in half lengthwise. Tie it around the soufflé dish, allowing it to extend 3 inches above the rim. Use ½ tablespoon of the butter to grease the inside of the foil strip. Dust the inside of the dish and the foil strip with 2 tablespoons of the sugar.

In a heavy saucepan, melt the remaining butter and whisk in the flour. Cook for 2 minutes. Stir in the chocolate over low heat until it melts. Add the milk to the pan, stirring quickly until smooth. Stir in the cup of sugar and cook, stirring until thickened. Beat with a whisk for a minute or two. Remove from the heat and scrape into a very large bowl.

Whisk in the egg yolks, two at a time, and the vanilla. This much of the preparation can be done in advance. But if you are not going to use the chocolate mixture immediately, place a piece of plastic wrap directly on the surface to prevent a skin from forming.

Preheat the oven to 450 degrees. Set the soufflé dish in a large pan, like a roasting pan. Have a kettle of boiling water ready.

Beat the egg whites with the cream of tartar, slowly at first to incorporate as much air as possible. Increase the speed and beat until the whites hold peaks but are still creamy. Fold 2 large spoonfuls of the egg whites into the chocolate mixture to lighten it. Fold in the rest of the egg whites.

Spoon into the prepared dish. Place in the oven and add hot water to the outer pan. Bake 40 to 45 minutes. Remove the collar, sift the confectioners' sugar on top, and rush to the table.

My Mother's Pavlova

THIS RECIPE HAS BEEN PASSED DOWN FROM MY MOTHER, VERONICA LOUISE WHITE, WHO WAS BORN IN AUSTRALIA, TO ME AND MY SISTER. THE DESSERT WAS SUPPOSEDLY CREATED TO HONOR THE BALLERINA, ANNA PAVLOVA, WHEN SHE VISITED AUSTRALIA. IT'S SIMPLY A BIG MERINGUE, WHICH IS USUALLY SERVED WITH FRESH BERRIES AND WHIPPED CREAM.

4 LARGE EGG WHITES, AT ROOM TEMPERATURE

1 CUP SUGAR

1½ TEASPOONS WHITE VINEGAR

3 CUPS RASPBERRIES OR SLICED STRAWBERRIES OR A MIXTURE OF BERRIES

1 CUP HEAVY CREAM, WHIPPED

6 TO 8 SERVINGS

Preheat the oven to 250 degrees. Trace an 8-inch circle on a piece of parchment and place the parchment on a baking sheet.

Beat the egg whites until very frothy. Continue beating, gradually adding the sugar, until the egg whites are very stiff. Beat in the vinegar.

Spread the meringue in the circle, making it higher around the edges, almost like a tart shell. The meringue should be about an inch thick on the bottom of the circle. Place it in the oven and bake 2½ hours. Turn off the heat and allow it to cool in the oven.

When the meringue is cool, use a spatula to release it from the paper and place it on a serving dish. Set aside at room temperature until ready to serve.

Spread berries in the center of the meringue, top with the whipped cream, and serve.

A mixture of berries is always terrific on the Pavlova. But other fruit, including diced tropical fruit (mango, banana, pineapple, kiwi) with a splash of rum would be excellent. Any cracking that occurs in the meringue will be masked by the fruit and whipped cream so do not worry! The Pavlova can also be baked as individual meringues, 4 inches in diameter.

Lemon Squares

*T*HESE LEMON SQUARES ARE AMONG MY ALL-TIME FAVORITES. MY MOTHER ALWAYS HAD A TREAT LIKE THESE FOR ME WHEN I CAME HOME FROM SCHOOL. THE BEST GADGET FOR GRATING CITRUS ZEST IS A MICROPLANE OR SIMILAR BRAND. THIS RELATIVELY NEW KITCHEN TOOL IS RAZOR-SHARP AND EFFECTIVE, SO YOU CAN EASILY SWIPE OFF ONLY THE VERY OUTER LAYER OF THE SKIN, WHICH IS WHERE THE FLAVOR AND OILS ARE CONCENTRATED.

½ POUND (2 STICKS) UNSALTED BUTTER, SOFTENED

2 CUPS PLUS 4 TABLESPOONS ALL-PURPOSE FLOUR

½ CUP CONFECTIONERS' SUGAR, PLUS MORE FOR DUSTING

2 CUPS GRANULATED SUGAR

1 TEASPOON BAKING POWDER

4 LARGE EGGS

6 TABLESPOONS LEMON JUICE

3 TEASPOONS GRATED LEMON ZEST

Preheat the oven to 350 degrees.

Blend the butter, 2 cups of flour, and the ½ cup confectioners' sugar together and press firmly into a 9 x 13-inch glass baking dish. Bake for 20 minutes, until set and very lightly colored. Set aside to cool.

In a bowl, whisk together the remaining 4 tablespoons flour, the granulated sugar, and the baking powder. Beat the eggs just until blended and add the lemon juice and lemon zest. Stir in the sugar and flour mixture until well blended.

Pour onto the cooled crust and bake for another 30 minutes, until set.

Allow to cool completely, sift confectioners' sugar over the top, then cut into squares.

ABOUT 24 SQUARES

This recipe is a near-classic: a shortbread cookie crust baked with a
kind of lemon curd. But as an after-dinner pastry, the lemon squares
are delightful because they are not too sweet. If you have a small
cake stand, serve the lemon squares piled up on it.

ANNE GRAUSO

Aunt Julie's Sugar-Crusted Brownies

MY SISTER JULIE IS A TALENTED COOK AND HER BROWNIES ARE ALWAYS A CROWD-PLEASER. THE BROWNIES KEEP EXTREMELY WELL IN AN AIRTIGHT CONTAINER AND THEY CAN ALSO BE FROZEN. THE MORE ELEGANT THE OCCASION, THE SMALLER YOU SHOULD CUT YOUR BROWNIES.

3/4 POUND (3 STICKS) UNSALTED BUTTER, PLUS MORE FOR PAN

3 1/2 CUPS SUGAR

8 OUNCES HIGH-QUALITY UNSWEETENED CHOCOLATE (99 PERCENT CACAO)

6 LARGE EGGS

2 TEASPOONS VANILLA EXTRACT

2 CUPS ALL-PURPOSE FLOUR

1 CUP CHOPPED WALNUTS, OPTIONAL

Preheat the oven to 350 degrees. Butter a large, 12 x 17-inch jelly-roll pan and dust with about 4 tablespoons of the sugar.

Place the chocolate and remaining butter in a saucepan over low heat. Cook, stirring occasionally, until both are melted. Remove from the heat.

In a large bowl, beat the eggs and remaining sugar just until blended but not frothy. Stir in the vanilla. When the chocolate mixture is no longer hot, slowly pour it into the egg mixture, stirring. Stir in the flour. Fold in the nuts, if desired.

Spread the batter in the pan and bake 35 minutes, until set. A toothpick inserted in the middle will come out just about clean. Allow to cool completely before cutting.

These days there is very high-quality unsweetened chocolate sold in
many stores. It pays to use it instead of the everyday supermarket
variety, which tends to have a gritty texture.

Millionaire Turtles

T HIS RECIPE HAS BEEN IN MY FAMILY FOR YEARS. MY MOTHER MADE THESE TURTLES FOR ME IN ATLANTA, WHEN I WAS GROWING UP, AND NOW I MAKE THEM FOR MY CHILDREN IN NEW YORK. I LOVE TO HAVE GOODIES LIKE THESE IN THE HOUSE SO MY CHILDREN KNOW THAT WHEN THEY BRING THEIR FRIENDS OVER, THEY WILL FIND A YUMMY SNACK. I LOVE IT WHEN A BUNCH OF TEENAGERS RAIDS THE REFRIGERATOR. CUT THE TURTLES IN UNIFORM PIECES AND DO NOT HESITATE TO INCLUDE THEM ON A COOKIE PLATE TO SERVE WITH COFFEE AFTER DINNER.

I CUP CHOPPED WALNUTS

³/₄ POUND (3 STICKS) UNSALTED BUTTER, SOFTENED

2 CUPS ALL-PURPOSE FLOUR

I ³/₄ CUPS DARK BROWN SUGAR

3 TABLESPOONS HEAVY CREAM

6 OUNCES HIGH-QUALITY SEMISWEET CHOCOLATE
(65 TO 70 PERCENT CACAO), CHOPPED

ABOUT 50 SQUARES

Preheat the oven to 350 degrees.

Toast the walnuts on a baking sheet in the oven or in a dry skillet on top of the stove.

Pulse ½ pound (2 sticks) of the butter, the flour, and 1 cup of the sugar in a food processor 10 to 15 times or until crumbly. Press the mixture evenly into a 9 x 13-inch baking pan. Bake for about 25 minutes or until light golden brown. Remove from the oven to cool.

Scatter the nuts over the pastry.

Stir together the remaining ¼ pound (1 stick) of the butter, the remaining sugar, and the cream in a heavy 2-quart saucepan over low heat for 4 minutes or until the butter is melted and the mixture is blended into a caramel sauce. Pour the caramel over the nuts on the pastry and spread it over the surface. Return the baking pan to the oven and bake for 20 minutes. Scatter the chocolate on top. Return to the oven for about 3 minutes, so the chocolate melts. Use the back of a fork to spread the chocolate over the top.

Chill for 1 hour until firm. Cut into 1½-inch squares.

These turtles can be made without nuts or, for variety, with pecans or even with salted peanuts.

Coconut Macaroons

THESE ARE MY VERY FAVORITE COOKIES. MY MOTHER BAKED THEM FOR ME WHEN I WAS A CHILD AND SHE CONTINUED TO MAKE THEM WHEN I WAS IN MY TEENS, SENDING THEM TO ME OVERNIGHT BY MAIL AT SCHOOL. SHE EVEN PRESENTED ME WITH A BOX OF THEM WHEN I MOVED INTO MY FIRST APARTMENT—WITH THE RECIPE ATTACHED. SO I WAS REALLY ON MY OWN.

14 OUNCES SWEETENED SHREDDED COCONUT
1 CAN (14 OUNCES) SWEETENED CONDENSED MILK
1 TEASPOON VANILLA EXTRACT
2 EXTRA-LARGE EGG WHITES, AT ROOM TEMPERATURE
1/4 TEASPOON KOSHER SALT

Preheat the oven to 325 degrees. Line a cookie sheet with parchment paper.

Combine the coconut, condensed milk, and vanilla in a large bowl. Beat the egg whites and salt on high speed in the bowl of an electric mixer until they hold medium-firm peaks. Fold the egg whites into the coconut mixture.

Using 2 teaspoons, form small mounds, about 1½ inches in diameter, placing them about 2 inches apart, on the cookie sheet.

Bake for 25 to 30 minutes, until golden brown. Cool before serving.

ABOUT 30 COOKIES

These are real New York macaroons, the kind that Jewish households serve on Passover.
Since the major supermarket brands of sweetened condensed milk and sweetened
coconut are certified kosher and even kosher for Passover, you can make these instead
of opening a can. For a very professional effect, pipe the batter from a large star tube.

JUDITH WINSLOW

Chocolate Chip Cinnamon Oatmeal Cookies

THE ORIGINAL RECIPE FOR THESE COOKIES CAME FROM A FRIEND IN WILLIAMSBURG, VIRGINIA. I MADE MY OWN ADJUSTMENTS. I ADDED CINNAMON, ELIMINATED THE SALT, AND INCLUDED OATMEAL FOR NUTRITION AND TEXTURE. I BAKE THESE COOKIES AT A MOMENT'S NOTICE. IN FACT, IN THE WEEKS AFTER SEPTEMBER 11, I WOULD BAKE ABOUT 6 DOZEN OF THEM AT A TIME TO GIVE TO A FRIEND, A NURSE, TO TAKE TO THE FIREMEN WHO WERE WORKING AT THE WORLD TRADE CENTER SITE. THE COOKIES WERE A HIT, AND I RECEIVED A VERY TOUCHING NOTE FROM THE FIREMEN AFTERWARDS—AND AN OFFICIAL COMPANY SWEATSHIRT.

1/4 POUND (1 STICK) UNSALTED BUTTER, SOFTENED

1/2 CUP GRANULATED SUGAR

1/2 CUP LIGHT BROWN SUGAR

1 TEASPOON VANILLA EXTRACT

1 LARGE EGG

1 CUP ALL-PURPOSE FLOUR, SIFTED

1 TEASPOON BAKING SODA

2 TEASPOONS CINNAMON

6 OUNCES SEMISWEET CHOCOLATE CHIPS, ABOUT 1 CUP

1/3 CUP REGULAR, NOT QUICK OR INSTANT, OATMEAL

Preheat the oven to 350 degrees. Line two cookie sheets with parchment or use a little of the butter to grease them.

Cream the butter and sugars together. Add the vanilla and egg and mix until smooth. Whisk the flour, baking soda, and cinnamon together in a bowl and stir into the batter. Stir in the chocolate chips and the oatmeal.

Drop scant tablespoons of the batter on the cookie sheets, spacing them 2 inches apart.

Bake for 12 to 15 minutes, according to your preference for light or darker cookies. If both sheets cannot fit in your oven at the same time, simply bake one after the other. Remove from the oven, allow cookies to cool on the baking sheets for 10 minutes, and then remove them with a spatula to a rack or racks to continue cooling. Allow them to cool completely before eating.

An elegant dinner party is not the occasion for serving these cookies. Then again, perhaps it is. They will make everyone happy. As an alternative, bake them and give two to each departing guest in a small plastic or cellophane bag for a generous and gracious touch.

ALISON BARR HOWARD

My Nanny Anna's Crescent Cookies

ANNA TOOK CARE OF ME WHEN I WAS LITTLE. SHE WAS A TINY WOMAN, FROM AUSTRIA. ON FRIDAYS, WHEN I CAME HOME FROM SCHOOL IN TIME FOR LUNCH, SHE WOULD ALWAYS HAVE THESE COOKIES FOR ME AS A TREAT. THEY ARE A KIND OF SHORTBREAD, BETTER THAN ANY OTHER.

1 CUP CHOPPED PECANS OR WALNUTS

2 1/2 CUPS ALL-PURPOSE FLOUR

1/2 CUP CONFECTIONERS' SUGAR

1/2 POUND (2 STICKS) UNSALTED BUTTER, SOFTENED, PLUS MORE AS NEEDED

1 TEASPOON VANILLA EXTRACT

1 CUP SUPERFINE SUGAR

ABOUT 40 COOKIES

Preheat the oven to 325 degrees. Line 2 baking sheets with parchment.

Place the nuts in a food processor and pulse until finely ground. Add the flour, confectioners' sugar, and the butter to the work bowl of the food processor. Add the vanilla. Process until well blended and the mixture clumps into a dough. Add a little more butter, about a tablespoon, if needed to form a soft, pliable dough that is not sticky.

Form the dough into a log. Then take pieces of the log, about an inch and a half in diameter, and roll them into small cigar shapes; then bend them to shape into small half-moon cookies.

Arrange the cookies on the baking sheet. They can be no more than an inch apart because they will not spread.

Bake them for about 25 minutes, until the tops are barely colored and the bottoms are golden brown. Immediately sprinkle them heavily with the superfine sugar. Turn them to coat both sides. Allow the cookies to cool on racks.

Shortbread crescent cookies are not only Austrian, they are also made in Greece, Mexico, and in the American South. These cookies keep very well and, before the finished cookies are rolled in sugar, they can be frozen. Sugar them after defrosting.

Vera's Farina Halvah

THIS RECIPE CAME FROM MY GRANDMOTHER, WHO WAS FROM GREECE. I LOVED EATING THIS HALVAH AS A CHILD.

2 CUPS SUGAR

1/2 POUND (2 STICKS) UNSALTED BUTTER

3/4 CUP PINE NUTS

2 CUPS FARINA, NOT INSTANT, PREFERABLY WHOLE WHEAT

Place sugar in a saucepan with 2 cups water. Bring to a boil, stirring once or twice, until the sugar dissolves. Simmer for 10 minutes. The mixture will register about 200 degrees on a candy thermometer. Set aside.

Melt the butter in a large, heavy saucepan. Add the nuts and cook over medium-low heat, stirring, until the nuts are lightly browned. Gradually pour in the farina and cook, stirring, until the farina has colored slightly.

Slowly pour in the sugar syrup, mixing constantly. Continue to cook over medium heat until the mixture is thick and easily lifts off the bottom of the pan, about 10 minutes from the time you start adding the syrup.

Spread the halvah in a 9 x 13-inch baking pan and allow to cool, then cut or scoop it into balls or other shapes.

NOTE: Whole wheat farina produces a nuttier-tasting confection than does white farina.

8 SERVINGS

VERA'S FARINA HALVAH CANDY, A VARIATION

BY COOKING THE MIXTURE LONGER, TO ABOUT 240 DEGREES, IT WILL HARDEN AS IT COOLS AND TURN INTO A BRITTLE-LIKE CANDY.

ABOUT 1 1/2 POUNDS

2 CUPS SUGAR

1/2 POUND (2 STICKS) UNSALTED BUTTER

3/4 CUP PINE NUTS

2 CUPS FARINA, NOT INSTANT, PREFERABLY WHOLE WHEAT

Place sugar in a saucepan with 2 cups water. Bring to a boil, stirring once or twice, until the sugar dissolves. Simmer for 10 minutes. The mixture will register about 200 degrees on a candy thermometer. Set aside.

Melt the butter in a large, heavy saucepan. Add the nuts and cook over medium-low heat, stirring, until the nuts are lightly browned. Gradually pour in the farina and cook, stirring, until the farina has colored slightly.

Slowly pour in the sugar syrup, mixing constantly. Cook over medium heat until the mixture is thick and easily lifts off the bottom of the pan, then continue to cook it until it reaches about 240 degrees. Drop a small amount of this mixture into a glass of very cold water. It should harden. If not, cook it a little longer.

Spread the mixture in a 10 x 15-inch jelly-roll pan. It will be thin. Allow it to cool completely, then break it into pieces as you would peanut brittle. Store in a plastic bag.

Teaspoon-size balls of the halvah can be put into little fluted candy cups, like the ones used for truffles. Serve them with tea or coffee, or on a cookie plate. They are also delicious alongside ice cream or sorbet.

Panda Bear Cupcakes

THESE CUPCAKES ORIGINATED AS A PROJECT IN THE DEPARTMENT OF PEDIATRICS. WE MAKE THEM WITH PATIENTS AND THEIR SIBLINGS. THE CHILDREN VOTED FOR THIS AS THEIR FAVORITE RECIPE TO SUBMIT FOR THE COOKBOOK. THE PANDA BEAR CUPCAKES ARE ALWAYS A WINNING PROPOSITION!

3 CUPS ALL-PURPOSE FLOUR

1 TABLESPOON BAKING POWDER

1 TEASPOON SALT

2 CUPS GRANULATED SUGAR

1/2 POUND (2 STICKS) UNSALTED BUTTER, SOFTENED

3 LARGE EGGS, AT ROOM TEMPERATURE

2 1/4 CUPS MILK, AT ROOM TEMPERATURE

3 1/2 TEASPOONS VANILLA EXTRACT

1 CUP UNSWEETENED COCOA, PREFERABLY DUTCH PROCESS

1 1/2 TEASPOONS WHITE VINEGAR

3 CUPS CONFECTIONERS' SUGAR, DIVIDED

2/3 CUP HEAVY CREAM

Preheat the oven to 350 degrees. Line twenty-four 2½-inch cupcake tins with paper liners.

Whisk together the flour, baking powder, and salt. With an electric mixer, cream the sugar and butter until they are light and fluffy. Beat in the eggs one at a time.

Mix the milk with 2½ teaspoons of the vanilla extract. Add the flour mixture to the butter mixture alternately with the milk in three batches, beating just until blended to make a smooth batter.

Transfer 2½ cups of the batter to another bowl and mix in ¾ cup of the cocoa. Stir in the vinegar.

By teaspoonsfuls, drop the vanilla batter alternately with the chocolate batter into the cupcake cups, filling them about three-quarters full. Do not stir. Place in the oven and bake 25 to 30 minutes, until a cake tester comes out clean. Remove from the oven and set aside to cool.

While the cupcakes are cooling, whisk 2 cups of the confectioners' sugar in a bowl. Add 5 to 6 tablespoons of the cream and mix until well blended. Stir in the remaining 1 teaspoon of the vanilla. In a small, separate bowl, whisk the remaining cup confectioners' sugar with the remaining ¼ cup of the cocoa. Add 2 to 4 tablespoons of the cream, adding a little more if needed to make the mixture spreadable.

When the cupcakes have cooled, ice each with half vanilla, half chocolate icing, making a pattern, like putting two small circles of chocolate icing on the vanilla, like a panda's eyes. Allow to set, then serve.

Cupcakes will remain fresher if they are baked in fluted paper cups. They are easier to unmold, serve, and eat that way. The panda-pattern icing is not required. Try putting a circle of chocolate in the middle, and then surrounding it with a border of white icing. Take the point of a knife and "pull" the chocolate icing into the white at ¼-inch intervals, going around the cupcake.

Menus

COCKTAIL BUFFET
Asian Ratatouille Spread
Parmesan Crackers
Society Salmon Mold
Baked Spinach Risotto
Palm Springs Chile Con Queso
St. Barth's Chicken Brochettes
My Nanny Anna's Crescent Cookies

SPECIAL OCCASION DINNER
Bruschetta with Pears and Blue Cheese
Blushing Crab Soup
Iceberg Wedges with Blue Cheese Dressing
Aunt Janet's Perfect Beef Tenderloin
Timbales of Smashed Garlic Potatoes
Fine-Tuned Green Beans with Feta
Petits Pots de Crème au Chocolat

SPRING BRUNCH
Maryland Crabmeat Spread
Accademia Lemon Spaghetti with Shrimp
Asian Asparagus Stir-Fry
Dutch Baby with Strawberries

SUMMER DINNER PARTY
Pond Water
Ali's Chilled Minted Pea Soup
Avocadoes Argentina
Sea Bass on the Grill
Herbed Orzo with Toasted Pine Nuts
Warm Corn and Prosciutto
Chocolate Soufflé

PICNIC PARTY

Sparkling Clear Sangria
Old-School Tomato Sandwiches
Sweet-and-Sour Meat Loaf
Perfect Potato Salad
Colorful Chinese Coleslaw
Summer Corn Salad
Aunt Julie's Sugar-Crusted Brownies
Lemon Squares

LADIES' LUNCHEON

Paris Iced Tea
Rainbow Goat Cheese Terrine
Favorite Tomato Soup
Chicken Salad for the Ladies
Rhubarb Cake

FAMILY PARTY

Warm Spinach and Boursin Cheese Dip
Melissa McGraw's Potato Chip Chicken
Martha's Vineyard Kidney Bean Casserole
Summer Squash and Zucchini Casserole
Mother's Macaroni and Cheese
Chocolate Chip Cinnamon Oatmeal Cookies
Panda Bear Cupcakes

OPEN HOUSE BUFFET

San Diego Frozen Margaritas
The New Cobb Salad
Scalloped Oysters
Yanna's Moussaka
Mushrooms with Pine Nuts
Creamed Artichoke-Spinach Casserole
Bermuda Banana Pudding

WINTER DINNER-BY-THE-FIRE

Pub-Style Cheddar Chutney Croustades

Hearty Lentil Soup

Chicken Cacciatore

Swiss Chard and Potatoes

Texas Pecan Pie

CHRISTMAS EVE

Swedish Christmas Glogg

Indulgent Spiced Pecans

Spanakopita

Cider-Roasted Loin of Pork

Nutted Wild Rice

Sweet Potato and Apple Casserole

Pumpkin Cheesecake

Millionaire Turtles

Acknowledgments

The Society of Memorial Sloan-Kettering Cancer Center wishes to thank Rizzoli Publications—most especially Charles Miers for his vision and belief in this project, as well as Christopher Steighner and Jonathan Jarrett for their incisive wisdom and guidance. It has been an honor to work with Florence Fabricant—we thank her for her inspiration, interpretation, gracious support, and so much more. Patricia Fabricant and Ben Fink have created a beautiful book that reflects our collective love of entertaining family and friends. Without this incomparable team, this would not have been possible. Thanks also to Holland Acres, Fischer & Page LTD., and Leontine Linens for their support.

We also give our sincere thanks to Vera Safai, the President of The Society of Memorial Sloan-Kettering Cancer Center from 2005 to 2007, for believing in this project and guiding us through the production of the cookbook, and to Leslie Jones, who as incoming President of The Society will wholeheartedly support us through its national launch.

—THE SOCIETY OF MEMORIAL SLOAN-KETTERING CANCER CENTER

A cookbook requires teamwork. For sourcing and testing the recipes to develop a manuscript, establishing the design that makes the text come alive on the page, commissioning the artwork and photography, and, finally, scheduling the marketing, many hands are inevitably involved. *Park Avenue Potluck* is a perfect example.

The members of the cookbook committee of The Society of Memorial Sloan-Kettering Cancer Center were involved in every detail, with Kelsey Banfield doing the heavy lifting. She was always there with needed material and a quick response to queries. From the start, The Society's dedication to this project facilitated my work.

I could, of course, count on Richard Fabricant's willingness to sample the scores of recipes I tested over three months of intensive cooking.

And for helping to test the recipes I am indebted to Sylvie Bigar's efficiency, enthusiasm, and fine palate. Though her expertise is French cooking, she easily found merit in the likes of grits, green chilies, grilled shrimp, and lemon squares.

Everyone at Rizzoli Publications—especially Charles Miers, the publisher; Christopher Steighner, the editor; Jonathan Jarrett, the editorial assistant; Pam Sommers, the publicity director; and Jennifer Pierson, the sales and marketing director—had a clear vision for this book, never wavering in their enthusiasm. They had the good sense to hire my daughter, Patricia Fabricant, to design it, making this our third joint venture, always a pleasure.

Ben Fink's skilled photography and Melissa Hamilton's styling contributed to the book's elegance and originality. And the generosity with which members of The Society opened their homes for photo shoots, lent their dinnerware and accessories, and hauled massive bouquets of fresh flowers up and down Park Avenue, made this book the best example of potluck I know.

Most important, I would like to take this opportunity to acknowledge an incomparable friend, Niki Singer Sheets. She was a great confidante—and she shared my enthusiasm for this project. I offer my contribution to this book in her memory.

—FLORENCE FABRICANT

Conversion Chart

All conversions are approximate.

LIQUID CONVERSIONS

U.S.	METRIC
1 tsp	5 ml
1 tbs	15 ml
2 tbs	30 ml
3 tbs	45 ml
¼ cup	60 ml
⅓ cup	75 ml
⅓ cup + 1 tbs	90 ml
⅓ cup + 2 tbs	100 ml
½ cup	120 ml
⅔ cup	150 ml
¾ cup	180 ml
¾ cup + 2 tbs	200 ml
1 cup	240 ml
1 cup + 2tbs	275 ml
1¼ cups	300 ml
1⅓ cups	325 ml
1½ cups	350 ml
1⅔ cups	375 ml
1¾ cups	400 ml
1¾ cups + 2 tbs	450 ml
2 cups (1 pint)	475 ml
2½ cups	600 ml
3 cups	720 ml
4 cups (1 quart)	945 ml (1,000 ml is 1 liter)

WEIGHT CONVERSIONS

U.S./U.K.	METRIC
½ oz	14 g
1 oz	28 g
1½ oz	43 g
2 oz	57 g
2½ oz	71 g
3 oz	85 g
3½ oz	100 g
4 oz	113 g
5 oz	142 g
6 oz	170 g
7 oz	200 g
8 oz	227 g
9 oz	255 g
10 oz	284 g
11 oz	312 g
12 oz	340 g
13 oz	368 g
14 oz	400 g
15 oz	425 g
1 lb	454 g

OVEN TEMPERATURES

°F	GAS MARK	°C
250	½	120
275	1	140
300	2	150
325	3	165
350	4	180
375	5	190
400	6	200
425	7	220
450	8	230
475	9	240
500	10	260
550	Broil	290

Index

Pub-Style Cheddar Chutney Croustades,
46–47
Puddings:
  Banana, Bermuda, 224–25
  Rice, Baked, 226–27
Puff pastry:
  Cheese Tart from Italy, 60–61
  packaged frozen, 61
Pumpkin Cheesecake, 214–15
Puree of Peas and Watercress, 182–83

Q

Quail eggs, in New Cobb Salad, 82–83

R

Rainbow Goat Cheese Terrine, 52–53
Raspberries:
  Paris Iced Tea, 34–35
  Pavlova, My Mother's, 232–33
Ratatouille Spread, Asian, *38*, 44–45
Rhubarb Cake, 210–11
Rice:
  Baked Spinach Risotto, 104–5
  Chili Casserole, California, 110–11
  Pudding, Baked, 226–27
  Seasoned Party, 192–93
  Spanish Seafood Casserole, 120–21
Risotto, Baked Spinach, 104–5

S

St. Barth's Chicken Brochettes, 150–51
Salad accompaniments:
  Bruschetta with Pears and Blue Cheese,
    48–49
  croutons, 67

Parmesan Crackers, 50–51
toast rounds with Warm Spinach and
  Boursin Cheese Dip, 58–59
Salads, 79–91
  Avocadoes Argentina, 80–81
  Chicken, for the Ladies, *78*, 84–85
  Chinese Coleslaw, Colorful, 172–73
  Cobb, New, 82–83
  Corn, Summer, 178–79
  Iceberg Wedges with Blue Cheese Dressing,
    170–71
  mixing, 84
  Pasta, with Pesto, 88–89
  Potato, Perfect, 174–75
  Salmon Mold, Society, 90–91
  Turkey Tonnato, 86–87
Salmon:
  Mold, Society, 90–91
  smoked, in Rainbow Goat Cheese Terrine,
    53
Salt-Crusted Snapper from Barcelona,
  138–39
San Diego Frozen Margaritas, 28–29
Sandwiches:
  Maryland Crabmeat Spread as filling for,
    54–55
  Tomato, Old-School, 42–43
Sangria, Sparkling Clear, 32–33
Santa Barbara Seafood Stew, 142–43
Scallop(s):
  Coquilles St.-Jacques, 118–19
  Puffs for a Crowd, *38*, 56–57
  Santa Barbara Seafood Stew, 142–43
Scalloped Oysters, 116–17
Scalloped Tomatoes, Heirloom, 96–97
Scampi Buzara, *124*, 132–33
Sea bass:
  on the Grill, 134–35